DHSS IN CRISIS

Social Security – under pressure and under review

Edited by Sue Ward

CHILD POVERTY ACTION GROUP
1 Macklin Street, London WC2B 5NH

1 Macklin Street, London WC2B 5NH
ISBN 0 903963 83 3

The views expressed in this publication are the authors' and do not necessarily reflect those of CPAG.

CORRECTION

The author of Chapter 4, 'Flat Broke', is Sally Coetzee. Sue Ward, who is listed on contents page and page 41, edited Sally Coetzee's original report. The editor and CPAG apologise for any distress this may have caused.

Cover design by Susan Hobbs
Typeset by Nancy White
Printed by Calvert's, North Star Press (TU) Ltd, London

Contents

Notes on contributors

Janet Allbeson worked until recently in CPAG's Citizens' Rights Office.

Fran Bennett is CPAG's Deputy Director.

Jonathan Bradshaw is Director of the Social Policy Research Unit, University of York, and a former member of CPAG's Executive Committee.

Judy McKnight is DHSS Group Secretary for the Society of Civil and Public Servants, and a member of CPAG's Executive Committee.

Rick Middleton is Development Worker at CHAR (Campaign for the Single Homeless).

Nick Raynsford is Director of Shelter Housing Aid Society.

Adam Sharples is Senior Research Officer at the National Union of Public Employees, and a member of CPAG's Executive Committee.

Roger Smith is CPAG's solicitor.

Sue Ward is a freelance journalist specialising in pensions and social security, and a member of CPAG's Executive Committee.

Acknowledgements

The editor wishes to thank Fran Bennett, David Bull, Michael Hill, Ruth Lister and John Murray for their helpful and constructive comments at draft stage; and staff at CPAG, especially Hilary Arnott, Claire Furlong and Sue Lind, for preparing the manuscript for publication.

The editor and CPAG would also like to thank Sally Coetzee and the Birmingham Welfare Rights Group for letting us reproduce an edited version of their pamphlet *Flat Broke*, originally published in 1983.

Preface

When this book was first conceived, it was intended simply to examine the way in which the Department of Health and Social Security (DHSS) was coping — or not — with the crisis forced upon it by political pressure to cut benefits and administrative costs, at a time when, with the increase in unemployment, demand for benefits was rising. The need for CPAG to make this sort of examination was then thrown sharply into focus with the setting up of a series of detailed reviews on aspects of social security.

The first of these, on pensions, was announced in November 1983; this was quickly followed by three others — on housing benefit, benefits for children and young people, and supplementary benefit (SB). Social services secretary Norman Fowler suggested that they were the most thorough reviews since the Beveridge Report.

They are not, nor are they likely to be. The purpose of this book is to show the rationale behind the review process which Norman Fowler has set up — what has been called the hidden agenda — and to look at the history of the 'crisis' in the DHSS and the effects this is having on the poor.

Chapter 1, by Sue Ward, seeks to place this crisis, and the reviews prompted by it, within the wider political context. Adam Sharples, in Chapter 2, looks at the economic framework and the Treasury's attitude in more detail. In Chapter 3, Judy McKnight looks at the crisis in the administration of benefits from the point of view of a union official dealing with the day-to-day problems. Then, in Chapter 4, Sally Coetzee shows how the effects of this administrative crisis in one particular city, Birmingham, led to a long strike among DHSS civil servants. Chapters 5, 6 and 7, which cover housing benefit (by Nick Raynsford), single homeless people (by Rick Middleton), and benefits for children and young people (by Janet Allbeson), are intended as 'case studies' of the effects on particular groups of certain choices which the government has made, both within the DHSS and within other departments. Chapter 8, on the take-up of means-tested benefits, and Chapter 9, on the treatment of fraud, are, in a sense, two sides of the same coin. Jonathan Bradshaw and Roger Smith are both looking at the content and context in recent years of claimants' supposed 'right' to benefit. While Jonathan Bradshaw demonstrates that a 'right' to claim means-tested benefits has been tenuous and insubstantial, Roger Smith shows how great is the government's concern that those with no such 'right' might be receiving benefits.

Finally, the last chapter (and its appendix), by Fran Bennett, summarises the evidence submitted by CPAG to the reviews, and outlines our views on how they *should* have been conducted, and what they *should* say. Although these are, in a way, now matters of history, they should not be forgotten, for the detailed answers to the questions of the review teams are perhaps less important than what has gone before. The political debate both within and outside government circles appears not to be about what tinkering can or should be done within the system, but rather, whether to alter the system fundamentally — and if so, how? This book is intended to be a contribution to the debate, from the standpoint of those deeply concerned about welfare benefits and claimants' rights.

1. Introduction: the political background

SUE WARD

In his parliamentary announcement of the reviews, social services secretary Norman Fowler set a high target for them. 'Taken together,' he said, 'the various reviews and studies I have set in hand constitute the most substantial examination of the social security system since the Beveridge Report 40 years ago.'[1]

He might find it useful to read the history of the Beveridge Report before making this sort of statement. Beveridge was working as a civil servant in the Ministry of Labour when he was asked to set up an interdepartmental review of Social Insurance and Allied Services, primarily to look at the anomalies that had arisen in the pre-war system. He interpreted this as giving him a chance to plan the future of welfare spending after the Second World War had finished. Once he started exceeding his brief, his fellow civil servants felt unable to continue on the committee and he went on alone, to produce a report at record speed.[2]

So far, there is some resemblance to Norman Fowler's reviews, expected to report on a mammoth system in less than a year—a timescale which CPAG strongly condemned as unrealistic.[3] The subsequent history of the Fowler reviews, however, is unlikely to resemble the Beveridge Report. Beveridge produced a document which, for all its considerable faults, was visionary in its scope and fitted very closely with the mood of people tired of war, and determined that never again would there be poverty and want as there had been in the 1930s. The context in which he made his proposals was clearly spelt out:

> The policy for full employment outlined in this report is a policy of spending and doing. It is a policy of common action. If we attack with determination, unity and clear aim the four giant evils of want, disease, ignorance and squalor, we shall destroy in the process their confederate; the fifth giant of idleness enforced by mass unemployment.[4]

This comprehensive call for public spending is a far cry from the Fowler reviews. They cover only small parts of the welfare state and, from the start, their terms of reference appeared to preclude any reforms that involve spending more money on any one group of social security claimants without spending less on another.

Patchwork reviews?

The review of pensions, announced in November 1983, was initially seen as an interesting innovation; but before there had been time to assess it, the next review (of housing benefit) was set up. This was followed by two more, announced in April 1984, on supplementary benefit (SB) and on benefits for children and young people. In mid-May, a rather lower-key review of maternity benefits was added. There is also a survey of the *number* of people with disabilities — being carried out instead of a review because the Department of Health and Social Security (DHSS) appears to consider the information about who is disabled, and the kinds of disability from which they suffer, too unreliable even for its high speed policy-making.[5] Subsequently, a review of social services was announced, and there has been for some time a management review of the health services.[6]

It has been said, therefore, that there is no aspect of the DHSS that is being left unreviewed. However, the social security reviews, on the surface at least, cover only some benefits. They do not cover the adult unemployed, lone parents, the industrially injured, widows, or the sick, except in so far as they are recipients of SB or housing benefit or benefits for their children. And while the pensions review *is* looking at occupational benefits as well as state benefits, the others are concerned with only half the picture — in fact, far less than half, because no one is looking at the benefits of the national insurance system (although questions have been asked about whether its contributory basis is still valid today). Yet it is precisely because of the massive loopholes in this system that so many people have fallen through its net and instead have to rely on means-tested benefits. And, just as important, the reviews only look at social security benefits. Tax reliefs, which have been called 'fiscal welfare', are not covered.[7] Nor are many of the other means tests for which the DHSS and other departments are responsible.

It has become increasingly clear, however, that the reviews may not be as piecemeal as they seemed at first sight. The group of civil servants responsible for coordinating the reviews, for example, has been studying broader issues which cut across the different reviews — including the interaction of taxation and benefits.[8] The drawbacks to this method of widening the area of debate are twofold. First, the process is happening behind closed doors: the public does not have access to this central coordinating unit. Second, the inclusion of taxation as a relevant issue is strictly limited to particular aspects of the tax system only.

For example, Norman Fowler told the House of Commons in January 1984:

> In 1982, 60% of those receiving standard housing benefit were paying tax and 300,000 families among those receiving housing benefit were paying income tax averaging £7.40 a week while receiving housing benefit averaging £5.10 a week. A further 600,000 people were paying higher taxes than that while still receiving housing benefit. Our aim must be to move away from this financial merry-go-round towards a system that will allow people to keep more of their own money and enable the state to concentrate its help on those who really need it.[9]

In November 1984, he told the House of Commons, 'The government is considering and will consider their proposals in conjunction with tax; that has never been at issue and it would be absurd to do otherwise.'[10] Yet all the indications are that the government is *only* considering the tax system in terms of the low level of the tax threshold, and its significance as a contributing factor to the poverty and unemployment traps. Wider questions—such as whether the structure of the income tax system as a whole could be made fairer, or whether tax reliefs and allowances are an equitable method of distributing help from the state—do not seem to be being addressed. Indeed, the housing benefit review was specifically precluded from considering mortgage interest tax relief in its terms of reference.

The social security budget

This section looks briefly at the social security budget as a whole, to establish what it really covers. Social security benefits are one of the largest programmes, both in financial terms and for the numbers of people they affect. They now cost almost £40 billion a year, and account for almost 30 per cent of public expenditure.[11] More than 20 million people are direct beneficiaries. The chart below illustrates how the government planned to spend this money in 1984/85. Much has been made of the size of this budget, but what is less often made clear are the differences between the various sections and the *political* reasons why parts of it have grown so fast (as shown in Chapter 2).

Social security systems in virtually every country have at least three roles to fulfil. The chaotic arrangements in the UK mean that these roles are more confused than elsewhere, but nonetheless they do exist, and should be clearly spelt out.

First, there is the role of *transferring* income between different groups of the population. The bulk of this transfer takes place between the generations. The 43.3 per cent of the social security

How the money goes on the welfare state

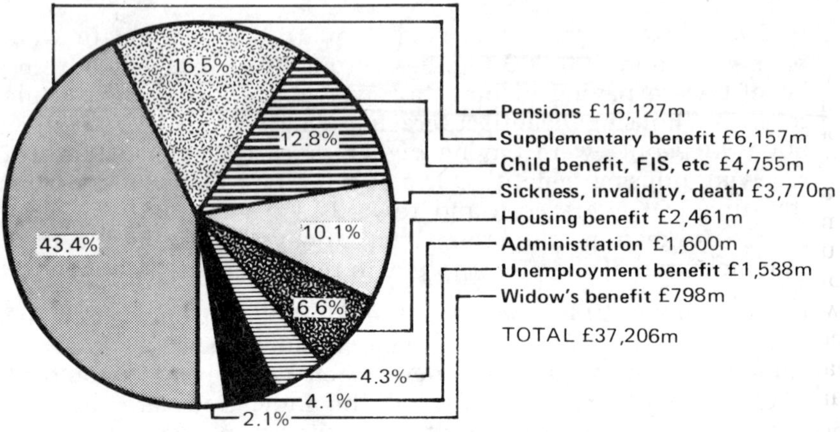

Source: The Government's Expenditure Plans 1984-85 to 1986-87, Cmnd 9143-II 1984, Table 2.12

budget that goes on pensions is the largest single example. Society, it could be said, has decided that those who have had a working life time should be supported collectively by the next generation. The system of national insurance contributions and pensions, in particular, is thus largely a method of collecting money from one generation and handing it back to the previous one. Some of those who receive national insurance pensions are, in fact, better off than some of those who pay the contributions. It has been estimated that a fifth of working families have incomes below that of the average pensioner, and a tenth of pensioner households have an income above the average for working families.[12]

In discussions of the philosophy behind the welfare state, this transfer of income has been seen as a contract between generations. The working population accepts a responsibility to support the elderly population, partly because it considers this arrangement to be socially just, but partly out of self-interest, since it also wants to be looked after in its turn.[13]

Child benefit, 13 per cent of the social security budget, also falls into this category; it is money paid by society to assist with the cost of bringing up children. CPAG's own evidence to the review of benefits for children and young people developed this point further.[14]

The second role of the system is the *insurance* element, embodied in the term 'national insurance' that was used but not invented by Beveridge. CPAG has argued elsewhere that the contribution tests and benefit limitations currently incorporated in the British national insurance system are unfair and unnecessary;[15] but this does not alter the theoretical principle behind the system, that of *collective insurance against risk*. This role links in closely with the transfer element in social security provision. Society asks people to pay, both via national insurance and in tax, to support those who have fallen foul of the risks of life, such as unemployment, disability or widowhood—again on the assumption that they will be similarly cared for if they fall into difficulty.

The classification of what risks are covered and what are not is fairly arbitrary and owes much to past political decisions, often made on the basis of short-term expedients or cultural or moral judgments. Thus, for example, widowhood is insured against, but other forms of single parenthood are not. Or, take disability—which, until recently, attracted different benefit rates and different conditions for receipt of benefit according to its cause. By and large, the industrially injured were treated with most generosity, and congenitally disabled housewives with least. Changes made since 1979, and in particular the Health and Social Security Act 1984, have eroded these distinctions, although it is too early to say what the full effects will be.[16]

The third role of the social security system—carried principally by SB which accounts for 16.5 per cent of the total spending—is the *relief of poverty*. The SB system does this for those not in full-time work who have fallen through the holes in the transfer payments and insurance net. It also has to deal with those—a very large group—for whom national insurance benefits are inadequate by themselves, since these benefits have always been held at levels on which it is not possible to live without other income. For the working poor, there is a network of other benefits, overlapping and difficult to cope with, such as family income supplement and free school meals.

This threefold categorisation, though, takes no account of the 'fiscal welfare state'[17] of tax reliefs, which should certainly not be disregarded. Nor does it cater for a number of benefits which do not fit tidily into any category, of which housing benefit is the prime example.

The DHSS picks up the tab

The 'untidy' nature of housing benefit (HB)—and, indeed, its remarkably troubled history—can be largely attributed to the fact that it has been stretched to the limit in trying to do more than one job. As well as its primary function, for the DHSS, of helping people on low incomes with their housing costs, it has had to deal with the effects of decisions made in other departments of government. The resulting administrative and financial problems, however, lie where they fall—with the DHSS and the social security system.

This theme—of a 'DHSS in crisis' partly as a result of its 'safety net' function for other government departments and other policy areas—recurs in a number of chapters of this book.

Thus, the prime intention of the new HB system was to help people, both working and not working, whose living standards would fall below acceptable levels if they were not given assistance with the cost of housing and of local government rates. However, it was also called upon to mitigate the effects of policy decisions in a different area, that of rent levels. This meant compensating for the government policy of steadily increasing council house rents by providing a means of reducing those rents, on an individual basis, to those who would otherwise be unable to meet them. This secondary function has enormously increased the numbers of people claiming HB. (See Chapter 5 for details of the history of HB and the administrative difficulties since its introduction.)

The rising cost of HB, one of the reasons originally given for reviewing it, is thus a burden thrown upon the DHSS budget by other departments. Similarly, the increase in SB payments for the unemployed results from economic decisions by the Treasury and the Cabinet as a whole. Spending over a wide area of the DHSS's functions is 'demand-led': the DHSS has to respond to all those who request, and can prove their entitlement to, benefits. The demand is created, in many cases, not by chance but by policy decisions taken in other departments. Yet when increased demand leads to increased spending, it is often from within the DHSS and the social security system that a solution to the 'crisis' is expected.

Consensus threatened

It is the threefold role of social security, outlined above, that CPAG now fears is under threat, not only from the reviews, but also from outside groups who may have some influence on the government. The previous consensus view of the system, recently described in the *Financial Times* as 'a reasonable if unintended, compromise between three different approaches to social security . . . the insurance, means test and universal benefit routes',[18] is in danger of being replaced by a view that the only legitimate role for the welfare state is the relief of poverty (via means-tested benefits). The crisis in the administration of benefits (outlined in succeeding chapters of this book) is paralleled by a crisis of confidence in the underlying philosophy of the social security system.

Thus a number of those giving evidence to the review of benefits for children and young people were questioned on their views about 'the' role of the welfare state. In CPAG's case, as soon as the magic words 'the relief of poverty' had been uttered, the chairman interrupted before further roles could be mentioned.[19] Among groups on the far right, the Adam Smith Institute has asserted that 'the present benefit system in fact hurts the poor by spending valuable resources on those who do not really need them'; and that the system of providing pensions via a transfer of resources from one generation of workers to the previous generation 'has been uncharitably, but perhaps accurately, likened to a chain letter, with its attendant morality and its likelihood of future collapse'.[20]

Among those seen as more 'middle of the road', the Institute for Fiscal Studies, in a widely publicised report,[21] similarly dismissed income transfers between generations and the provision of collective insurance as functions which the state should not perform.

Thus, some groups seem to be attempting to bring about a shift in the consensus by arguments which concentrate only on the poverty-relieving role of social security. This view of the system, of course, gives means-tested benefits a central place in welfare state provision. Yet, when pointing to the shortcomings and difficulties of the current social security system — and sometimes suggesting that nothing could be worse — these and other groups often do not add that many of these problems are centred in precisely those means-tested elements which they wish to extend.[22]

The three agendas

Within the government, different sections want the words of the reviews to mean different things. The 'agendas' can be crudely divided into three:

- the DHSS agenda: the short-term expedients,
- the Treasury agenda: the public spending 'problem',
- the agenda of the right-wing ideologues.

The DHSS

First of all, the reviews are another recognition of the crisis into which the DHSS has been moving steadily for years — another attempt at reconciling the political pressures for a reduction in costs with the escalating demand for services. That there is a crisis of administration in the DHSS cannot be doubted. Two recent publications by CPAG, on the SB and HB schemes, have spelt this out, and they have been corroborated by a number of other independent reports.[23]

The SB scheme was already cracking in the 1960s, and David Donnison, when he became Chair of the Supplementary Benefit Commission in 1975, saw an urgent need for reform. The 'scrounger-phobia' that was apparent in the media and in parliament during the late 1970s (as described by Roger Smith in

Chapter 9) gave additional impetus to the pressure for change—for different reasons.

However, Donnison expected reforms to be made in a context in which at least some people would have been 'floated off' SB. In the 1970s it was predicted that, with fewer pensioners relying on SB because of the introduction of the new earnings-related pension scheme, the number of claimants would fall over the following decade. This has not happened. Although fewer pensioners are relying on SB, the overall number of people dependent on SB has still increased—from 4.4 million in 1975 to 7.2 million by August 1983.[24]

It is the massive growth in unemployment which has pushed up the numbers so dramatically. Between the end of 1979 and December 1982, the number of unemployed claimants leapt from 560,000 to 1.7 million, and the cost of their benefits from £705m to £4,865m.[25] The long-term unemployed are a rising proportion of the total numbers of unemployed, and for them the SB scheme, which restricts them permanently to the short-term rate, is singularly ill-equipped. It is more complex, and more administratively expensive, to pay benefit to the unemployed than to pensioners, whose circumstances do not change very much over the years. So the figures hide an even sharper increase in the actual burden of administration.

At the same time as this sharp increase was happening, the government was pushing through a whole series of changes in benefit structures and administrative arrangements, of which the Social Security Act 1980 was only the first instalment. Civil servants have had little time to find out the faults and problems arising from one set of changes, before being asked to move on to the next. Because of the complexity of the system, each change in one area affects others. Since 1980 there have been introduced, among other things:

- postal SB claims for the unemployed;
- statutory sick pay;
- housing benefit;
- a number of computer experiments;
- changes to the appeals and adjudication process;
- cuts and changes in national insurance benefits, including the abolition of earnings-related supplement.

Yet all this has had to be dealt with by a DHSS staff which has increased at a far slower rate than has the number of claimants. In 1979 there were 96 SB claimants to every one staff member. In 1984 there were 129[26]—and this ratio includes more than 1,000 DHSS staff members employed as extra fraud detection workers,[27] rather than on paying out benefits. (The effect of these pressures on the staff is graphically detailed in Chapter 3; and the breakdown and strike which resulted in one city (Birmingham) is outlined in Chapter 4.)

Thus, the reviews take their place in a long line of attempts to change the system, going back to the setting up of an officer review team which published *Social Assistance* in 1978[28] — and, indeed, before that. The DHSS has for years been engaged in 'crisis management' of the social security system.[29] There has been a series of administrative responses to the growing demands on the scheme, and the increased complexity required to cope with them. These responses have failed because of a *political* refusal to spend enough money to carry through the reforms properly.

A good example of this was the 'legalisation' of SB under the 1980 Social Security Act. This converted the SB system from one in which many decisions were based on the discretion of the officers, without a framework of case law or legal precedents, to one in which decision-making is tightly circumscribed by detailed regulations.

CPAG, and others in the poverty lobby, had for years criticised the tangled and uncertain discretionary arrangements, under which the claimants had few rights and little chance to find out what rules were being applied in their cases and why. Discretion, it was argued, should be placed within the context of a clear and easily understood framework of law. Today, we have got the framework of law, but it is neither clear nor easily understood. It was pushed through at speed, with few resources diverted to staff training,[30] and it was used in a number of instances as a chance to cut benefits by codifying the rules in a tight, indeed rigid, way. What should have been of benefit to claimants has turned into a disaster.

Much the same has happened with the HB scheme, where the rational idea of unifying the various systems for giving assistance with housing costs has turned into an administrative nightmare, carried out as it was on the basis of no extra spending. Yet the social security system is in such a mess that a serious and just reform *cannot* take place without extra money being spent. As Geoffrey Beltram, himself a former senior civil servant at the DHSS, has said of the SB scheme:

> The supplementary benefit scheme is not effective enough in its operation to justify leaving things as they are. Solutions to the basic problems—the relationship between the scale rates and the structure of entitlement and AR [additional requirements] and SP [single payments], the problem of take-up generally, quality of service and the responsiveness to cases of exceptional need—cannot be cost-free.[31]

It is this basic truth that the Conservative government, like some of its predecessors, has refused to grasp. They have continued to look for a magic key which will enable them to do everything at once — simplify the system, reduce staff, save money and have a fair and rational system which looks tidy and can be justified to critical outsiders. They cannot have all those things at once and, time and again, when the politicians and civil servants realise this, what has been sacrificed is the interests of claimants — those for whom the system should surely be designed.

The current reviews are but the latest in a long line of fruitless searches for an easy answer. These include the 1966 Social Security Act, which altered National Assistance to supplementary benefit; the 1973 Report of the Fisher Committee,[32] which was set up by a previous Conservative government to report on the level of fraud and abuse in the system; the 1978-9 Review, set up by Stan Orme when he was Secretary of State, which resulted in the report *Social Assistance* and the 1980 Act; and the Rayner review of benefits for the unemployed in 1981.[33] And each new search for a solution has to take into account the effects of previous 'reforms'.

The Treasury agenda

Running alongside this role of the reviews—as a short-term expedient to find ways of solving problems largely created by similar 'cobble-ups' in the past — lies the Treasury's desire to contain public spending in the long term. It appears that the reviews were put forward by Norman Fowler partly in order to 'buy off' the Chancellor's demands for cuts in the DHSS budget during the 1983 and 1984 public expenditure survey committee (PESC) processes.[34] It is in the nature of short-term postponements of this sort that sooner or later the day of reckoning arrives.

If the Treasury is to achieve its goal of containing public spending, and therefore cutting taxation in any substantial way, it cannot leave unscathed the social security system which accounts for 30 per cent of the public expenditure planning total. Nor can it content itself with nibbling at the means-tested elements in that 30 per cent, since they account for less than a fifth of it.[35] To achieve what is sought by large sections of the government, and by the monetarists within the Treasury, it will be necessary to attack the major spending programmes, of child benefit and national insurance benefits such as pensions, and reduce either the size of the benefits paid or the numbers to whom they are paid.

Chancellor Nigel Lawson's Green Paper on public spending makes this clear.[36] The Green Paper's key argument is that public spending must not be allowed to rise in line with the output in the economy. Public spending might match inflation, or even grow a little in real terms, as long as it decreases as a share of the national income. Government should first decide which programmes can or should be afforded, and then set the spending plans. The section on social security specifically says that there is no 'right level' for benefits; they have to be related to each other and to the total amount of money available. (See Chapter 2 for how the government's policy on this has evolved, and the background against which it must be seen.)

There are other groups — for instance, much of the actuarial profession and the Institute for Fiscal Studies — who, while not necessarily supporting the Treasury's simple cost-cutting approach, are convinced that some cuts will have to be made in the future. As Fran Bennett wrote in April 1983:

> There is a growing body of opinion which claims that, in the next 20 or 30 years, the 'dependency ratio' will become so unfavourable that the costs of even current benefit commitments will be unacceptable. The 'dependency ratio' means the numbers of 'economically inactive' people in relation to the numbers of employed people. Projections of the worsening dependency ratios have been used in particular to highlight a potential crisis in the new state pensions scheme, as it reaches maturity, and full benefits start being paid simultaneously with an increase in the number of pensioners. It is then argued that those in employment may not accept the high level of deduction necessary to support those out of the labour market.[37]

The statistical horror stories miss the point that what matters is the overall level of national wealth and how it is distributed, not the numbers of people engaged in producing it. They contain a grain of truth, however, in that *if* we have a stagnant economy for the next half century, with unemployment remaining at its present level or rising, *and* our present regressive and arbitrary system of taxation and benefits, there will be a problem; and public resentment towards the system, and towards claimants, will probably grow. The solution to the problem, though, lies with the government's economic and taxation policies, as much as with its social security policy.

The Treasury's intention appears to be that the reviews will provide justification for 'reforming' the social security system in ways that will cut costs in the long term. One interpretation is that the reviews are, in part, the outcome of a long Cabinet battle over the social security budget. Norman Fowler, while by no means a 'wet', has fought fairly hard to protect his empire. He has been supported by others within the Cabinet who are aware of the vote-losing potential of an attack on the more popular parts of the system such as pensions. In the 1983 round of public spending cuts, not long after the election, the DHSS budget was hit, but by no means as hard as the Treasury wished.

The price of this short-term reprieve, however, seems to have been the concession of a long-term review of costs. The pensions inquiry, announced in November that year, was the first indication of such a review. In April 1984 the *Sunday Times* reported that subsequently a group had been set up within the Cabinet to work out a way of cutting benefits without creating public hostility. 'It was this group', according to the report, 'which in February approved Fowler's own suggestion that the spending options should be aired through detailed reviews.'[38] Perhaps as a result of understandings reached at this stage, Norman Fowler has consistently refused to rule out the possibility of any 'savings' being used to finance tax cuts, although implying at the same time that the reviews are not a cutting exercise.[39]

The ideological agenda

The mechanistic view held by sections of the government, that public spending on social security (or anything else) is bad in itself, and therefore to be reduced, is reinforced by far-right monetarists and 'supply-side' economists, such as the Adam Smith Institute and the Institute of Economic Affairs (IEA). Groups such as these believe that the state ought not to be in the business of income redistribution at all, as this 'interference' with the free market pushes wages up and reduces individual freedom. Dr Rhodes Boyson, a DHSS minister at the time when the reviews were instituted, wrote in 1978, 'Conservatives must actively work for the welfare state to wither away as personal freedom and independent provision take its place.'[40]

An example of this line of thinking comes from Professor Patrick Minford of Liverpool University, one of the first to give oral evidence to the review of benefits for children and young people. His blueprint for the future, published in the IEA journal,[41] involves dismantling all state unemployment and disability insurance and pension provision and handing them over to private enterprise. He would retain the SB system, but at a level that 'excludes all items not necessary for survival'; and unemployed workers would have their benefits 'capped' so that no one could receive benefit higher than 70 per cent of their net income from their last job. Child benefit would be raised, so that parents could meet the cost of health and education — which would be entirely privatised — themselves. This arrangement would be complemented by a negative income tax system, under which people would be granted a certain level of income *on condition* that they took out the prescribed kinds of insurance. The reasoning behind these proposals is that Britain is pricing itself out of the market, and therefore out of economic prosperity, by the combination of high wages and high public spending. Minford regards up to 60 per cent of government expenditure as a 'pure burden of waste on our society' because of the 'inefficient' ways in which it is channelled. He therefore regards this as a major contributory factor to the unemployment level. If public spending was reduced, and the supposed disincentive effect of the current level of benefits abolished, he believes that employment would rise by 2½ million.

Cuts and changes in the social security structure, therefore, are being urged on the government in furtherance of its long-term economic policy by some of those proffering advice from the far right. They appear to have the ear of the Prime Minister, and of members of her private office, such as John Redwood, who are in a position to influence policy. This is not to suggest, however, that there is a monolithic ideological outlook within the government. The electoral pragmatism of a number of Cabinet ministers, and their concern for their own departments, is presumably why some of the cuts demanded by the Treasury in the past have been rejected—and why any proposals for major cuts in social security which might arise from the reviews are likely to meet opposition not only from outside the government but also from within.

References

1 *House of Commons Hansard*, 2 April 1984, cols 652-60.
2 Jose Harris, *William Beveridge: a biography*, Clarendon Press 1977.
3 Letter to *The Times* (dated 26 June 1984), jointly with a number of other organisations.
4 Beveridge, *Social Insurance and Allied Services*, 1942, Cmnd 0404, para 385.
5 *House of Commons Hansard*, 2 April 1984, col 653.
6 DHSS press release, 25 October 1984, on the terms of reference of the management review set up in February 1984.
7 For a classic discussion of this, see R Titmuss, *The Social Division of Welfare: some reflections on the search for equity, an essay on the welfare state*, George Allen & Unwin 1958.
8 J Walpole, 'Current social security issues', *Politics Today*, Conservative Research Department October 1984, pp 315-16.
9 *House of Commons Hansard*, 19 January 1984, col 469.
10 *House of Commons Hansard*, 8 November 1984, col 232.
11 *Chancellor's Autumn Statement*, HM Treasury, November 1984, Table 2.1.
12 *Population, pension costs and pensioner income: background paper to pensions review*, HMSO 1984.
13 See, for example, *Report of the Phillips Committee on the Economic and Financial Problems of Provision for Old Age*, 1954, Cmnd 9333.
14 Published in *1984: Changed Priorities Ahead? CPAG's evidence to the social security reviews*, CPAG 1984.
15 See G Fimister and R Lister, *The Case Against Contribution Tests*, CPAG 1980.
16 See *Rights guide to non-means-tested benefits*, 7th edition, CPAG 1984, Section 2 for an explanation of the changes under the Social Security (Severe Disablement Allowance).
17 See Titmuss, note 7 above, who also defines a third system (not covered

here): the 'occupational' or 'workforce' welfare state, which consists of 'fringe benefits' provided by employers for their employees.

18 Michael Prowse, *Financial Times*, 30 August 1984.

19 Transcript of evidence, 10 September 1984 (unpublished).

20 *Social Security Policy*, Omega Report, Adam Smith Institute 1984, pp 4 and 22.

21 A W Dilnot, J A Kay, and C N Morris, *The Reform of Social Security*, IFS 1984.

22 See, for instance, Dilnot et al, note 21 above, pp 1, 42, 113.

23 J Allbeson and R Smith, *We don't give clothing grants any more*, CPAG 1984; and B Clark, J Daly and J Douglas, *Nobody's Benefit: a survey of the housing benefit scheme*, CPAG 1984. See also G Beltram, *Testing the Safety Net*, Bedford Square Press 1984; and R Berthoud, *The Reform of Supplementary Benefit*, Policy Studies Institute 1984, on the SB scheme; and National Association of Citizens' Advice Bureaux, *Housing Benefit: the cost to the claimant*, 1984, and Greater London Association of Citizens' Advice Bureaux, *Housing Benefit: a case of irretrievable breakdown?*, 1984.

24 *House of Commons Hansard*, 25 January 1983, cols 601-2W, and DHSS, *Social Security Statistics 1975*, HMSO.

25 *Sunday Times*, 8 April 1984.

26 Allbeson and Smith, note 23 above, p 12.

27 Allbeson and Smith, note 23 above, p 12.

28 DHSS, *Social Assistance: a review of the supplementary benefit scheme in Britain*, 1978.

29 C Walker, *Changing Social Policy: the case of the supplementary benefits review*, Bedford Square Press 1983.

30 Berthoud, note 23 above.

31 Beltram, note 23 above.

32 *Report of the Committee on Abuse of Social Security Benefits*, Cmnd 5228, March 1983.

33 Department of Employment and DHSS, *Payment of Benefits to Unemployed People*, HMSO March 1983.

34 *Sunday Times*, 8 April 1984.

35 Figures from *Chancellor's Autumn Statement* (see note 11).

36 HM Treasury, *The Next Ten Years: public expenditure and taxation into the 1990s*, Cmnd 9189, March 1984.

37 *Poverty*, no 54, April 1983, pp 13-14.

38 *Sunday Times*, 8 April 1984.

39 In a briefing for journalists immediately after announcing the reviews; and in oral evidence to the Social Services Select Committee (*Fourth Report from the Social Services Committee*, July 1984, p 163).

40 R Boyson, *Centre Forward*, Temple Smith 1978, p 123.

41 *Institute of Economic Affairs Journal*, April-June 1984 supplement.

2. Costs and benefits: **the economics of social security**

ADAM SHARPLES

In January 1984 Prime Minister Margaret Thatcher, in an interview with the London correspondent of the *New York Times*, took the opportunity to unburden her fears about the growing cost of the welfare state. Britain, she warned, faced a 'time bomb' over social security spending, and the consequences of the present arrangements should be brought before the British people 'before it is too late'.[1]

The interview took place against the backdrop of persistent scares, promoted by the Conservatives, that Britain is heading for a 'fiscal crisis' — a massive imbalance between the claims for public spending and the revenues available to support it. For example, in June 1982 *The Times* leaked details of a pessimistic report prepared by an 'interdepartmental group of officials' on the outlook for public spending and taxation in the coming decade.[2] The report, which was presented to the Cabinet in the autumn of 1982, warned that, if the economy remained stagnant, tax increases equal to 15 pence in the pound on income tax could be needed to balance the books in the 1990s.

More evidence of the government's preoccupation with the cost of the welfare state came when *The Economist* revealed that, following the interdepartmental committee's work, a paper had been circulated to the Cabinet from the Central Policy Review Staff (the Think Tank) advocating radical surgery on public services to allow room for the tax cuts that it considered necessary to boost the economy.[3] It suggested ending all state funding of higher education, replacing the National Health Service with private health insurance and freezing spending on all social security benefits in cash terms.

The more moderate members of the Cabinet, with one eye on the impending election, successfully blocked discussion of the paper, but there is little doubt that its ideas were fed into the lengthy internal debate on future prospects for spending that took place throughout 1983. In early autumn 1983 there were further press reports about likely cuts as the public expenditure review process got under way. One outcome of these debates was the

Green Paper entitled 'The Next Ten Years: public expenditure and taxation into the 1990s'.[4]

After the heat of the earlier exchanges, the Green Paper itself must have been a disappointment to the prophets of budgetary doom. Slipped out under the cover of Budget day publicity, it was largely descriptive. Projections into the future identified no great problems, and the conclusions were—on the surface—bland and reassuring. As long as public spending was held roughly constant in real terms, there would be some scope for reducing 'the burden of taxation'.

The Green Paper, however, followed several years of rumoured and actual cuts in social security spending. When, therefore, social services secretary Norman Fowler announced the 'most fundamental review of the social security system since Beveridge',[5] observers could be forgiven for suspecting that knives were being sharpened.

Social security looms large

It is not difficult to see why social security spending should loom large in the minds of those preoccupied with a belief in the impending fiscal crisis of the welfare state. It is by far the largest spending programme. At nearly £40 billion, it is larger than the defence, health and housing budgets put together.[6]

Social security has also been one of the fastest-growing spending programmes in recent years. Ten years ago, it took up just over 20 per cent of total public spending. It now forms more than 30 per cent of the total and, under existing plans, its share will rise by a further one per cent in the next three years.

To a government committed to cutting public spending, the burgeoning social security budget must be a source of constant chagrin. In the Green Paper, the government conceded that its plans to slim down the public sector had achieved little. Public spending rose by 7 per cent in real terms between 1978/79 and 1983/84. The parallel economic collapse pushed up government spending as a proportion of national output from 42 to 46 per cent. Social security spending over this period rose in real terms by 26 per cent. On a crude measure, ignoring the impact of programmes which were cut in real terms, social security accounted for 94 per cent of the total real increase in spending over the period.

To those 'far-right' ideologues dreaming of a world without welfare, the last straw is that social security spending is not subject to neat packaging and control. Cash limits control roughly half the spending by central government and the central contribution to local government spending. The government decides what should be spent in cash terms and, with rare exceptions, these limits are adhered to. Spending without cash limits (for example, that on family doctors) is determined by demand. Social security makes up three-quarters of all the central spending without cash limits.

Putting these factors together—the size of the programme, its rapid growth in recent years and the apparent lack of control—it is easy to see why those who see public spending as a problem soon pick on social security. Are these fears justified? Can we afford the social security programme we may like to see on social grounds? To put the debate in perspective, we need to step back a pace or two and start to unravel the arguments.

The public spending 'problem'

The first knot to disentangle is what exactly is the public spending 'problem' that the government and its economic advisers make so much of? It is important to understand that there are several definitions of the problem, based on different sets of assumptions, although the conclusions often overlap.

The first definition focuses on the level of public borrowing—the gap between spending and tax revenue. Monetarists argue that a high level of borrowing will mean raising funds from the banking system, which, in turn, will tend to boost the money supply. A growing money supply then causes—by some mechanism on which monetarists can never quite agree—a rising price level.

In this version, therefore, the 'problem', a large deficit, can be dealt with either by raising taxes or cutting spending. In practice, this government has done both. Despite its populist election pledges, it has increased the overall tax take from 34 per cent of national output to 38 per cent.[7] Public spending *plans* have been cut back, but the actual level of spending has risen.

It could be demonstrated at length that there is little or no validity in this account of the problem; but this need not concern us here since, if it is a problem, it has been 'solved'. Once the deficit has been reduced, as it has, to levels the government finds acceptable, public spending can be allowed to grow in line with the growth in tax revenue. With no change in tax rates, revenues will grow roughly in line with the growth in the economy.

The second definition concentrates on the *level* of public spending and the taxation required to support it. According to this approach, popular with the Confederation of British Industry, Chancellor Nigel Lawson and drafters of White Papers on local government finance, Britain has been held back by burdensome and inhibiting levels of tax. The only way to get the economy moving, it is said, is to make drastic cuts in welfare spending, thus allowing for tax cuts to release the spirit of enterprise and initiative.

There are some rather obvious difficulties with this. Britain has a lower level of public spending, in relation to national output, than any other Common Market country except Greece.[8] Nor has anyone yet demonstrated why a lower level of tax should encourage anyone to work harder or manage more efficiently than they do now. There is simply no mechanism to link lower tax and better economic performance.

In the first phase of the present Conservative government, the advocates of radical tax cuts to reinvigorate the 'supply side' were overshadowed by the macro-monetarists who wanted tax increases to lower the fiscal deficit. But they were not beaten, and their views resurfaced strongly in the Think Tank report of 1982.

An interesting new variant of the 'supply side' case for spending cuts has appeared in recent government thinking and features prominently in the Green Paper. Reduced tax levels are no longer advocated as the *precondition* for growth, but as the *reward* of fiscal virtue and economic success. Lower tax is assumed to be desirable in itself. So, providing public spending can be held down in real terms, the extra tax revenue generated by higher output can be used to finance lower tax rates. The Green Paper offers the hope that, 'If the public expenditure planning total is held flat (for the next ten years), the burden of non-North Sea tax could be brought down to well below its 1978-79 level of 34½ per cent by 1993-94.'[9] This case for spending cuts or limitation rests on a simple ideological preference rather than economic reasoning.

The third approach is concerned, not so much with the current balance between spending and tax or the long-term level, as with the *trends* in tax revenue, on the one hand, and growing demands for spending, on the other. Roughly, the argument is that, without any change in policy, there are likely to be considerable pressures to increase spending on certain services. The government is committed to a steady rise in spending on defence and law and order; public service workers are likely to demand a rise in their living standards; new technology is likely to increase demands for spending, for example, in the National Health Service; and rising numbers of dependants—particularly the elderly and unemployed—are going to push up spending on health and social security.

On the tax side of the equation, revenues from the North Sea are likely to fall steadily from their current peak—from £8½ billion in 1983/84 to £5½ billion in 1993/94 at 1982/83 prices, according to the Green Paper. If steady growth does not materialise as promised, then there will not be the revenues to meet growing pressures on spending without an increase in tax rates. A recent article in the *Daily Telegraph* (23 April 1984) put these fears bluntly:

> The cost of social security is rocketing both in the amount of cash spent ... and when expressed as a percentage of total public spending. The average worker already pays more than a quarter

of his [sic] income in tax and it is estimated that unless the spiralling cost of public spending is halted, the proportion will rise to one half by the year 2000. The main reason for the continually growing cost of social security is that there are proportionately fewer workers supporting a growing army of dependants.

This argument is in many ways the most dangerous, because it lays claim to some economic, or at least demographic, rationale in advancing the case for cuts. To tackle the argument, it is necessary to look at the social security budget—its current shape and size, recent trends and future prospects—in more detail.

Where the money goes

Total planned spending on social security for the financial year 1984/85 is £38,391m, of which £1,184m is spent in Northern Ireland. Spending within Great Britain breaks down as shown in Table 1.

Table 1: *Public spending on social security in Great Britain 1984/85*

	£m	*%*
Contributory benefits	20,699	55.6
Non-contributory benefits	14,907	40.1
Total benefits	35,606	95.7
Total administration	1,600	4.3
Total programme	*37,207*	*100*

Source: The Government's Expenditure Plans 1984-85 to 1985-86, Cmnd 9143-II, HMSO 1984, Table 2.12.

Administrative costs, which are split between the DHSS, the Department of Employment and local authorities, make up less than 5 per cent of the programme. Within spending on benefits, contributory benefits form the larger part, but the share of non-contributory benefits has risen, from 24 per cent in 1973/74 to 31 per cent in 1978/79 and to 40 per cent today.[10]

Almost half of all social security spending goes on the elderly, as Table 2 shows. The unemployed and families with children claim a further third, split equally between them; and the disabled and long-term sick claim one-tenth.

Table 2: *Benefits divided by broad groups of beneficiaries* 1984/85*

	£m	*%*
Elderly	18,260	49.3
Unemployed	6,540	17.6
Family	6,360	17.2
Disabled and long-term sick	4,270	11.5
Widows and orphans	1,090	2.9
Short-term sick	350	0.9
HB to those in work	190	0.5
Total	*37,060*	*100*

Source: Cmnd 9143-II, Table 2.12.3.
*Includes SB and HB paid to claimants in each group. The figures include rate rebates which are not part of the definition of public spending used above.

Recent trends

We have seen how the rapid increase in social security spending over the last decade has been used to encourage fears that spending is soaring out of control. A closer look at the trends helps to put the 'problem' in perspective.

Social security spending in cash terms has risen more than six-fold since 1973/74. When the rise in prices over the period is taken into account, the increase in 'real' spending is still substantial—68 per cent (calculated from Table 3). This increase is overwhelmingly the result of three special features.

• In 1977 child benefit was introduced for the first time, replacing family allowances and tax allowances for children. The latter were phased out gradually. By April 1979 the change-over was complete. It is estimated that the 'hidden' cost of child tax allowances in 1976/77 was £2,364m at 1982/83 prices.[11] The switch to child benefit simply made this cost explicit, so that it then counted as public expenditure.

• The 1970s saw a particularly rapid growth in the total number of pensioners. The total number of people entitled to retirement pensions rose from 7,750 million in 1973/74 to 9,260 million in 1984/85. This in itself would have boosted the cost of social security by 10 per cent, with no increase in the value of benefits. But this growth is almost at an end: the number of pensioners will rise by only 600,000 up to the end of the century.[12]

• Most important of all, unemployment has been pushed up to record levels. At the end of 1973, there were barely half a million

Table 3: *Public spending on social security*

	Total public spending on social security £m*	*As % of total public spending*	*Index of prices** 1982/83 = 100*
1973/74	5,824	19.9	28.9
1974/75	7,324	18.6	34.5
1975/76	9,925	20.3	43.2
1976/77	11,603	21.3	49.0
1977/78	13,905	24.3	55.7
1978/79	16,437	25.0	61.5
1979/80	19,417	25.2	71.9
1980/81	23,429	25.3	85.3
1981/82	28,567	27.3	93.8
1982/83	32,445	28.6	100
1983/84	35,324	29.4	105.0
1984/85	37,207	29.4	110.2
1985/86	39,520	29.9	114.5*
1986/87	41,630	30.5	119.1*

Source: Public Expenditure White Papers (various years); *House of Commons Hansard*, 6 June 1984, col 183; *Economic Trends* (various issues).
*Based on government assumptions.
**GDP deflator for financial year, calculated by averaging quarterly index.

registered as unemployed. By the end of 1975, nearly a million had been added to this figure. In 1979 the Conservatives reversed two years of steady decline in the jobless total and added nearly two million to the dole queues in their first five years. The cost, in unemployment benefit, supplementary benefit (SB) and housing benefit (HB) for the unemployed soared from an estimated £364m in 1973/74 to £1,370m in 1978/79 and £6,540m in 1984/85.[13] These figures do not include the massive cost in lost tax through unemployment and the price tag for special employment and training schemes. Neither do they include the knock-on effects of unemployment on poverty in old age.

The balance of spending between different groups of beneficiaries is set out in detail in Tables 4 and 5. They show that these three factors — child benefit, the pensioner boom and unemployment — account for 69 per cent of the increase in social security spending over the last decade. They are factors which are unlikely to be repeated.

…reased social security costs 1973/4—84/5

	£m at 1982/3 prices	%
…cost of social security …—84/5	13,611	100
Cost … hild benefit (previously hidden as child tax allowance)	2,364	17
Extra cost due to increased number of pensioners	2,271	17
Extra cost due to unemployment	4,750	35
'Unexplained' increase in cost	4,226	31

Source: Calculated from Table 5.

The outlook for the future—the 'demand' side

Pressures for more spending on social security could arise from four factors:

- Demographic changes affecting the number of dependants, principally pensioners and children.
- Changes in the numbers entitled to benefits, owing to past or future policy changes.
- Economic conditions—low pay and unemployment—which make people dependent on benefits.
- Changes in the value of benefits.

Demographic changes

It is expected that the total number of people of pensionable age will rise from 10.1 million in 1981 to a peak of 10.5 million in 1991, before falling steadily to the end of the century. The proportion of pensioners in the population will be the same in 1994 as in 1984. The number of children is projected to fall by 0.3 million to the end of the decade, cutting the cost of child support.

The 'burden' of claims on social security is often measured by looking at the ratio between the dependent population—those of pensionable age plus children under 16 — and the population of working age. The projections in Table 6 confirm that this ratio is unlikely to be significantly higher in the year 2001 than in 1981, and it will 'improve' over the next decade. The improvement would be even more marked if the rise in the number of women of working age who are expected to move from the unpaid to the paid labour force was taken into account.

It seems ironic that we are told two horror stories about the future which are flatly contradictory. On the one hand, we are warned that there are going to be too few workers to support the cost of a growing army of dependants. On the other, the new

Table 5: *Benefits divided by broad groups of beneficiaries at constant 1982/83 prices (£m)*

	73/74	*74/75*	*75/76*	*76/77*	*77/78*	*78/79*	*79/80*	*80/81*	*81/82*	*82/83*	*83/84*	*84/85*	*85/86*	*86/87*
Elderly	11,085	12,068	12,593	12,796	13,285	14,276	14,089	14,232	15,192	16,020	16,571	16,525	17,013	17,330
Disabled	2,017	2,237	2,424	2,469	2,639	2,894	2,921	2,919	3,145	3,470	3,762	3,864	4,000	4,064
Short-term sick	1,237	1,186	1,153	1,163	1,203	1,171	946	809	768	620	324	317	323	327
Unemployed	1,169	1,220	1,983	2,276	2,460	2,228	2,045	2,966	4,371	5,160	5,867	5,919	6,009	6,045
Widows and orphans	1,203	1,288	1,288	1,183	1,131	1,122	1,057	996	1,002	1,000	1,010	986	987	991
Family	1,983	1,847	2,153	2,122	2,657	4,081	4,965	4,537	4,861	5,210	5,610	5,756	5,904	5,945
Housing benefit to people in work	—	—	—	—	—	98	97	117	160	170	171	172	166	168
Total	*18,694*	*19,846*	*21,594*	*22,009*	*23,375*	*25,870*	*26,120*	*26,576*	*29,499*	*31,650*	*33,315*	*33,539*	*34,402*	*34,870*

Source: Calculated from Public Expenditure White Papers (various years)

Table 6: *UK demographic trends*

	Population (millions)						
Year	(a) *Working age*	(b) *Under 16*	*as % of (a)*	(c) *Pension-able age*	*as % of (a)*	(d) *Total dependent population*	*as % of (a)*
1961	31.8	13.1	41	7.7	24	20.8	65.4
1971	32.3	14.2	44	9.0	28	23.2	71.8
1981	32.9	12.1	37	9.8	30	21.9	66.6
1991	34.7	11.8	34	10.4	30	22.2	64.0
2001	34.7	13.0	37	10.3	30	23.3	66.9

Source: Calculated from *Social Trends 1984*, No 14, HMSO 1984, Table 1.2.

technological revolution is going to mean that there are far too many people of working age to be gainfully employed in meeting our needs.

The truth, it will be no surprise, lies somewhere in the middle. Technological change generally increases the output per worker hour of those employed. The benefits of that change can be claimed in the wages or profits of those involved in production, in the increased leisure of the workers whose productivity is raised, or in the tax revenues to finance improved services and benefits. The choice between these is, in large part, political.

Entitlement to benefits

Entitlement to pensions is expected to increase as a larger number of married women become entitled to pensions in their own right. At present, some 800,000 people of pension age do not receive a pension.[14] The government estimates that the number of pensioners, as distinct from the number of people of pension age, will rise by 600,000 by the end of the century.[15] That is small compared with the rise of three million in the last 20 years.[16] Other changes in entitlement would derive from future changes in policy.

Economic conditions

These are the most difficult to forecast. The government's own prediction — or, more accurately, assumption — is that output will grow by 2¼ per cent in the five years up to 1988/89 and by between 1½ and 2 per cent in the five years thereafter (growth in the economy excluding oil production will be ¼ per cent higher).[17]

Many economists would see that as distinctly optimistic, given the record of the last five years and the government's continued commitment to tight fiscal and monetary policy. Even if these growth rates are achieved, the government is also assuming that increases in output per person 'will improve substantially' on those of the 1970s (1 per cent), but 'may not equal' those of the 1950s and 1960s (2.3 per cent).[18] However, if productivity rises at 2 per cent, and the labour force grows at ½ per cent a year, as expected, even economic growth of 2½ per cent would leave unemployment undented, as the growth in output per worker would mean there will only be a limited extra demand for workers.

The government's outlook, then, is for the jobless total to remain at least as high as it is today. This means that it can expect to see the unemployed taking about the same share of the social security budget. There could, of course, be further increases in unemployment if the current meagre growth rate is not sustained — for instance, if concern with inflation or balance of payments deficits causes the government to deflate the economy still more.

The value of benefits

This is largely determined by policy. The present 'neutral' policy is to increase most benefits each November in line with the rise in prices. Since 1983 the uprating has been based on the movement in prices in the year ending in May,[19] so there is no possibility of uncorrected 'overshooting'. Between 1975 and 1980, retirement pensions were increased in line with earnings or prices, whichever was rising faster, ensuring a long-term, though erratic, rise in the value of benefits.[20] With this provision removed, the only 'built-in' tendency for the value of benefits to increase arises from the state earnings-related pension scheme, launched in 1979.[21] Liabilities arising from the scheme will gradually build up until it reaches full maturity in 2023; but by the end of the century the additional cost of the scheme has been estimated at not more than £5 or £6 billion.

The general conclusion, then, is that there are no substantial in-built pressures increasing social security spending to the end of the century. If the value of benefits were held constant in real terms, the total bill would stabilise at its current level, falling steadily as a proportion of national income as the economy grows.

These projections are confirmed by the unpublished 'inter-departmental' paper circulated to the Cabinet in the autumn of 1982.[22] The paper considered two 'scenarios' ('A' and 'B' in Table 7 below). The optimistic view (A) was that growth would average 2½ per cent a year between 1980/81 and 1990/91. Even allowing for a 1 per cent growth in the real value of benefits each year, the total social security bill would rise by 7 per cent in real terms but *fall* from 11.3 per cent of gross domestic product in 1982/83 to only 9.7 per cent in 1990/91. On the pessimistic scenario (B), growth averages ¾ per cent for the first five years and ½ per cent for the second. *With benefits frozen in real terms*, the social security bill rises by only 2½ per cent over the eight years to 1990/91, while the share in output falls slightly.

Table 7: *Expenditure on social security—estimates*

	1979/80	*1982/83*	*1990/91* *(A)*	*1990/91* *(B)*
£m (1980/81 cost terms)	22,878	26,646	28,560	27,320
% GDP	9.6	11.3	9.7	11.1

Source: Confidential Report by Interdepartmental Group of Officials, 1982

Although this prospect sounds reassuring to the government and its supporters, the implications for the living standards of those who depend on benefits are appalling. Can it seriously be proposed that the standard of life of a substantial and generally deprived part of the population should be frozen over a period of decades, while the rest enjoy the benefits of the substantial economic growth we are promised? Yet it seems to be this prospect which guides the government's thinking.

Resources

The expected demands for benefits must be balanced against the resources available to fund them. The level of resources, from taxes on income, spending and capital and from national insurance contributions will rise almost exactly in line with the growth in the economy, as long as tax rates remain unchanged and allowances, thresholds and other limits are indexed to prices. Income tax revenue will increase slightly faster than income on this basis as real incomes increase and push more people over thresholds into higher tax bands. This effect will be offset (as noted on p 18) by a steady decline in revenues from North Sea activities after the mid-1980s.

The government's growth projections would increase the wealth of the economy by around 17 per cent between 1983/84 and 1990/91. Tax revenue would rise by a corresponding amount — generating an additional £20 billion.

On to the offensive

The result, as far as social security is concerned, is that the government is planning for a healthy *surplus* of revenue over expenditure. There is no crisis of exploding demands and contracting resources which demands urgent cuts. The only 'crisis' the government faces in the next decade is whether it can find enough money to give away in tax cuts before the next election. Indeed, before the government is allowed to go too far in its search for cuts, it should be pointed out that under the present 'medium-term financial strategy',[23] it has allowed for tax handouts — known in polite circles as 'fiscal adjustments' — amounting to £10 billion by 1988/89.

If the scare stories are dismissed, it may be possible to begin a more sensible discussion about the level of social security programmes that is desirable and affordable. Social security is about redistribution — transferring purchasing power, often from those in work to those outside. The stability of the system depends ultimately on the consent of the bulk of those who lose some income in the transfer, and, therefore, on some broad agreement on the right relation between the living standards of those in paid work and others.

If we start from the position that the present level of transfers through social security is broadly accepted, certain conclusions follow. With no change in tax rates, that part of tax and national insurance payments that finances benefits will rise as real incomes rise. If there is no adverse trend in the ratio of 'dependants' to 'paid workers' — and none is expected — then a neutral policy would be to increase the real value of benefits in line with real incomes over the last three decades of the century. Most people would probably agree that, over a period of time, the standard of living of pensioners, the unemployed and other groups should not be allowed to fall substantially behind the living standards of those in work.[24]

Guided by this principle, CPAG's argument that there is no economic or demographic case for social security cuts can only be a starting point. We need to establish that public spending plans for social security should be built on the right of all who are dependent on benefits to share in the rising wealth of the economy. On that principle, the cost of social security in relation to the economy would neither rise nor fall. We could, then, start to argue whether the scale of redistribution through social security should be increased and broadened and whether people are prepared to pay the scale of tax increases necessary to fund it. But we are a long way from that point in the debate.

To sum up, this chapter has tried to establish three key conclusions:

- The social security budget has risen rapidly in the last decade, from 20 per cent to 30 per cent of public spending, largely because of three factors: the switch from child tax allowances to benefits; the rising numbers of pensioners; and, most important, the soaring numbers of unemployed people.

• There are no major built-in pressures for more spending on social security for the remainder of this century, over and above the legitimate aspirations of those receiving benefits for a rise in their living standards, and the need to remedy clear deficiencies.

• There is no crisis of public spending, or social security spending, in the government's terms. There is no economic or demographic case for cuts. But those who depend on benefits for their living standards face a crisis of exclusion from the wealth of society if the government pursues its plans for a long-term spending squeeze.

References

1 Reported in *The Times*, 25 January 1984.
2 *The Times*, 30 June 1982.
3 *The Economist*, 18 September 1982.
4 Cmnd 9189, HMSO March 1984.
5 *House of Commons Hansard*, 2 April 1984, cols 652-60.
6 *Autumn Statement*, HM Treasury, November 1984, Table 2.1.
7 Cmnd 9189, HMSO March 1984, p 10.
8 *European Economy*, November 1983.
9 Cmnd 9189, para 59.
10 Public Expenditure White Papers—various years.
11 Calculated from *The Government's Expenditure Plans 1981/82 to 1983/84*, Cmnd 7841, p 111.
12 Cmnd 9189, para 31.
13 Public Expenditure White Papers, various years. Figures for 1973/74 are published only in 'survey prices' and not in cash. The cash figure is estimated.
14 *Social Trends*, HMSO 1984, *Social Security Statistics*, HMSO 1983.
15 Cmnd 9189, para 31.
16 *Social Security Statistics*, HMSO 1983 and 1974.
17 Cmnd 9189, Appendix 3.
18 Cmnd 9189, Appendix 3.
19 Social Security and Housing Benefits Act 1983.
20 Between April 1975 and April 1980 the value of the retirement pension rose by 16 per cent.
21 Social Security Provisions Act 1975.
22 Details of this were published in *The Times*, 7 October 1983.
23 *Financial Statement and Budget Report*, HM Treasury, March 1984, Table 2.6.
24 A similar point has been made by Conservative MPs, eg, John Maples and Tim Eggar, *House of Commons Hansard*, 6 March 1984, cols 804 and 807 respectively.

3. Pressure points: **the crisis in management**

JUDY McKNIGHT

As spelt out in Chapter 1, the social security system is now in crisis, and this has had an inevitable, and damaging, effect on the staff who have to administer it. The greater dependence on supplementary benefit (SB), which, as a means-tested benefit, is staff intensive, has led to greater pressure of work. At the same time, policies have been introduced which are aimed at cutting the cost of running the civil service and at cutting staff numbers.

The result of these policies has been a deterioration in the service and provision for claimants. The increasingly unacceptable working conditions for DHSS staff have led to a *less* efficient service, even though, for the government, 'efficiency' is a key concept. One issue which needs more attention from those who care about the welfare state is what this word 'efficiency' really means. The staff trade unions and CPAG might find it difficult to agree on a precise definition, because in some ways their interests are different. What is certain, however, is that they would not agree with the government's definition, since, for it, the reality is that 'efficiency' simply means staffing the civil service, and the DHSS in particular, in the cheapest possible way.

It is important not to equate social security with SB, and thus write the whole of social security off as being in crisis. The universal non-contributory benefits such as child benefit and maternity grant or the contributory benefits such as retirement pensions, unemployment benefit, invalidity benefit, widow's benefit or death grant, all have high take-up, relatively speedy service, are cheap to run and have a low level of consumer complaints. Their main flaw is that they are set at a generally inadequate level, and have not been adapted to meet new contingencies.[1] Similarly, family income supplement (FIS) is administered from Blackpool and has a very simplified, broad brush approach, which keeps its administrative costs low. Housing benefit (HB) has now been handed over to the local authorities, who, as Nick Raynsford describes in Chapter 5, are finding it extremely difficult to deal with.

Within the Department of Health and Social Security (DHSS)

itself, therefore, the main administrative burden comes from SB, the 'safety net' scheme. SB is having to bear large burdens as a result of government policies in other areas, especially the massive rise in unemployment and the cut in earnings-related supplement to unemployment benefit.

This chapter looks at the impact government policy has had, from the point of view of a person working full-time within a DHSS union. It discusses the staffing, administration and management policies since 1979, within the context of the priorities set for the DHSS. It then looks at the effect these developments have had in the local offices, and on the shape of the administration. Finally, it considers the opportunity new technology gives to improve the service for claimants — something that under this government seems increasingly unlikely.

More work, fewer staff

Since 1979 the workload of staff employed on SB work has increased dramatically. In May 1979 the total number of SB claimants was 3 million. By May 1982 this had risen to 4.15 million, and by May 1983 had reached 4.5 million.[2] This increase of 50 per cent in the total hides an even more dramatic increase in claims received from unemployed people, which has trebled since 1979, while the proportion of all SB claims which are from unemployed people has increased from 50 per cent to 67 per cent. While pensioners and other long-term claimants, once they are on benefit, tend to have relatively stable circumstances, many unemployed people go on and off benefit for short periods during the year, and even the long-term unemployed often have growing families whose circumstances change at frequent intervals, so that administering benefit for this group is considerably more time-consuming than doing the same for pensioners.

Comparisons between staffing and workloads over a period are difficult because of numerous procedural and benefit changes, but it is possible to make some measurement of the deteriorating situation. For SB, the staff/claims ratio of 1:100 in 1979 worsened by almost a third by 1983, to 1:132.[3] Since greater resources are now involved in the 'fraud and abuse' area, the burden on staff directly employed in paying out benefit is even larger than this measure would indicate. Thus, the ratio between staff actually paying benefit and the number of claimants has worsened by 38 per cent over the period 1979-83.

Since 1979 the number of staff in the DHSS has been cut by 8 per cent, from 98,000 to 90,000.[4] Some of the cuts have been made on a quite arbitrary basis; others have been justified by changes, such as those to HB, sickness benefit and the introduction of the postal claim form for unemployed people, that involved reduced labour requirements. However, each time, in the view of its trade unions, the DHSS has considerably overestimated the staff savings. For example, the DHSS trade unions have considered that the overestimate of 'savings' in statutory sick pay and HB alone was well over 900 posts.[5] Nor has there been any recognition that the process of changes to benefits and work procedures would add burdens in addition to the normal workload.

On a crude analysis of the extra workloads imposed by the changes in numbers of claimants, ignoring procedural changes, it is estimated that local office staffing should be 10,000 higher than it is today.[6] Yet the government has announced that between 1984 and 1988 the DHSS must lose another 3,000 jobs.[7] When asked by unions how these cuts will be made, the DHSS has said that no definite decisions have been taken, but that likely areas for 'savings' include legal aid, home visiting and a further extension of postal claim forms.[8]

The next sections look at the ways in which cuts have actually been carried out. In brief, these are: a squeeze on pay and conditions, a new emphasis on management techniques, and some heavy-handed attempts to save money through altering the way staff work.

Pay and conditions

The cuts in DHSS staffing—along with the rest of the civil service—are part of wider government policies aimed at running the civil service in the cheapest possible way. This means not just cutting staff numbers, but keeping pay to the bare minimum needed to recruit and retain staff and allowing working conditions generally to deteriorate.

After the government's unilateral decision in 1981 to abolish the system of pay research which determined civil service pay levels in relation to 'fair comparisons' with outside pay rates, civil servants in 1984 had a pay increase which meant that for the fourth year running they received less than the going rate in terms of outside settlements, and indeed less than the rise in the cost of living.

Other areas affected by the general cutbacks in running the civil service and the DHSS include training and accommodation. Training suffers particularly in over-stretched offices, where staff cannot be released because of pressures of work. Good accommodation has never been a feature of DHSS local offices, but the problem is currently made worse by the discovery of asbestos in many of them. Again, lack of cash due to spending limits has stopped this being dealt with quickly or efficiently, so that many local offices have been forced into industrial action over this issue.

Low pay and poor conditions of service lead to low staff morale. As any good manager knows, morale is vital for efficiency. This problem is compounding that of the increased workload and can only add to the difficulties of claimants.

Management techniques

In order to monitor and control public spending more tightly, the government has introduced a number of new management techniques into Whitehall, with names such as 'efficiency and effectiveness' and the financial management initiatives (FMI). *The Economist* of 17 November 1984 commented:

> Though each of these innovations is different, they share a vision of a new dawn of political programmes costed at the push of a button, priorities balanced and money saved—or at least better spent across the whole of the public sector.

Outside advisers, such as Sir Derek Rayner, have been brought in to help create a so-called efficient, streamlined civil service.

In attempting to run the civil service as if it were an industry, the government has been forced, however, to recognise that a department such as the DHSS could not be operated on the basis of the profit motive. As a substitute, the concept of 'financial management' was introduced in 1982. This works on the basis of delegating budgets to local managers, making them set objectives at the beginning of the year, and then building in incentives to ensure that objectives are met, and that budgets are not exceeded.

This sounds fine in theory, and could work in areas where work output is easily measured on a quantity basis. In the DHSS, however, work cannot — or should not — be measured purely on the throughput of cases. The quality of work and the level of service to claimants must also be considered. Financial management pays only lip service to measuring quality; it is designed primarily to measure quantity. Since quantity is easier to measure, quality gets left behind.

These new management philosophies multiply the effect of cuts. At a local level, all managers down to and including local office managers are expected to look for ways to run their own areas of operation in a cheaper way. Incentives are built in to ensure that managers aim to run their own work units, which have been labelled as 'cost centres', as cheaply as possible. An experimental system of financial control over local staffing has also been introduced in some offices. Under this system, known as 'manpower budgetary control', local office managers are encouraged to see whether their responsibilities can be discharged with fewer staff, or with lower grades.[9]

These objectives could be useful parts of an administrative procedure in a system with clearly defined goals. However, if they are themselves elevated to be the goal of the system, then they can distort the administrative process. The prime goal of the SB system should be to pay the proper amount of benefit to all people either claiming or entitled to claim, and to do so promptly and courteously. Currently, unacceptably high numbers of SB assessments are wrong (the official DHSS error rate stood at 10.5 per cent in 1983,[10] but independent assessments put the rate much higher[11]); delays in payment of benefit are escalating,[12] and there are huge problems of take up.[13] It is clear, therefore, that there is a fundamental malaise in the system.

Cuts have now become not just a government objective, but have been built into the heart of civil service management. Some of the wider implications of the effects of this in the DHSS deserve more public concern than they have so far received. For example, officials in the DHSS are under pressure to come up with ideas to save money, either on benefits or administration, especially ideas that do not involve an Act of Parliament. In this way, a slightly changed procedure for paying some benefits could limit costs without alerting either parliament or the public.

This raises questions about the extent of the accountability of civil servants to parliament, and through them to the electorate and the public generally. The introduction of 'merit pay' into the civil service for senior grades, in December 1984,[14] will only increase these pressures on management to find further ways of saving money for the government, at the expense of the claimant.

Financial management policies can also lead to complete management nonsenses. A classic example is the pursuit of policies which led to the strike by computer staff at the DHSS Newcastle Central Office in 1984. Through the computer installations at Newcastle and Washington, the largest non-military computer complex in Europe, the DHSS pays pensions and child benefit, and holds contributions records for the whole working population. The transfer from clerical ledger accounting to computerisation in the mid-1970s was a smooth and efficient operation—perhaps a model of how such a transition can be properly undertaken.

Until the arrival of financial management policies, the computer installation ran smoothly and efficiently and industrial relations among the staff were good. However, the introduction of these policies meant that management was under pressure to see how the computers could be run in a cheaper way. Under the Civil Service Shift Working Arrangement, an evening shift had to finish after 12.30am in order for the staff to qualify for 20 per cent shift disturbance allowance. If the shift finished before that, the staff only received 10½ per cent. In order to save an estimated £46,000 a year, management therefore proposed new shift working arrangements, with the evening shift finishing at 12.09am instead of 12.39am. The computer staff were expected to take a cut in take-home pay of as much as £50 per month.

Management's truculent insistence on forcing through these savings led to the civil service unions at Newcastle and Washington taking strike action. This strike lasted over six months and cost the government at least £100m in emergency procedures for pensions and child benefits,[15] in alternative arrangements for processing the uprating of benefits from November, and in recruiting 3,800 extra staff into local offices to cope with the extra pressures resulting from the strike. Massive extra expenditure—as yet unquantified—will also fall to the DHSS for the cost of keeping open post offices which would otherwise have been closed. No sensible industrialist would have considered it a sound proposition to risk over £100m, a major deterioration in efficiency for many years to come and a serious deterioration in staff relations and morale, for a meagre £46,000 per annum. The strike was ultimately successful in achieving the unions' major objective of protecting their members' take-home pay, so the costly industrial action did not even realise any substantial long-term savings for the DHSS department. There must be at least a suspicion that the dispute came about in the way it did partly because management decided to 'take on' a militant trade union group in the hope of defeating it and breaking its power—an aspiration which was unfulfilled.

Thus, concepts such as 'financial management' impede rather than assist improvements in quality of service. They build in a mechanism for continual cuts in a way which reduces accountability to the public. Ultimately, if the Newcastle strike is anything to go by, they do not necessarily achieve what they set out to achieve, and may increase rather than reduce public expenditure.

Efficiency and quality of service: the true measure

The government has tried in its cost-cutting exercises to demonstrate that the DHSS has been made more efficient in the process. In answer to a recent parliamentary question on efficiency in the DHSS, social services secretary Norman Fowler stated that there were two key indicators to measure efficiency: '(a) the unit cost of paying benefits, and (b) administration costs as proportion of total benefit expenditure'. He went on to say that the average unit costs of paying benefits fell by 4½ per cent in real terms between 1978/79 and 1981/82.[16] What his 'indicators' do not show is the fact that cuts in staff and other efficiency savings have only been made possible by a serious deterioration in the quality of service given by the DHSS.

In the past two years or so there has been a stream of independent publications criticising the deteriorating quality of service provided by DHSS local offices.[17] For example, the Family Service Unit[18] demanded an urgent overhaul of the entire benefit system, and complained about delays in processing claims, lost files, difficulties of telephoning the DHSS. It found that provision varied between offices, particularly with regard to single payments, and that free milk and vitamin vouchers were virtually unobtainable in some offices. The Greater London Citizens' Advice Bureaux survey[19] found that 40 per cent of clients were not receiving their correct entitlement due to errors by the DHSS. CPAG, in monitoring the 1980 supplementary benefit scheme, accepted that, given the major changes: 'A certain number of mistakes were unavoidable, but evidence of widespread dissatisfaction with the standard of administration is overwhelming' — 'From all our evidence we can only deduce that local offices simply do not have enough staff to do their job properly.'[20]

As all this evidence shows, staff cuts have meant not just reductions in the number of DHSS staff available to deal with the increasing complexity of means-tested benefits and the consequent pressures which have been caused in local offices. They have also involved reductions in home visiting, reduced verification and checking procedures and a range of other measures introduced under the superficially attractive jargon names of 'easement' or 'simplification' of the work. In practice, this has meant a considerable sacrifice of accuracy. Little account has been taken of the impact of this in terms of the need for time-consuming remedial action when errors are identified.

Delays in payment and errors in the amount of benefit paid have become increasingly common, and have caused a marked increase in telephone calls from the public.[21] Each phone call means stopping what one is doing and finding—or failing to find—the claim being referred to. So a residue builds up, and fewer and fewer claims can be dealt with speedily. Chapter 4, on the Birmingham strike, illustrates graphically how offices can reach breaking point.

The increase in telephone activity must also partly be a reflection of the policy of reducing home visiting. The ratio of visits to claims over the 1979-83 period has halved.[22] In addition to the planned cuts during 1983, 250,000 visits were 'abandoned' because offices were unable to handle these owing to the pressures of their other work.[23]

In theory, claimants are visited both to check claims for accuracy and to identify additional benefit entitlement. Reducing the frequency of visits or abandoning them altogether reduces the opportunities for claimants to explore the full range of benefits to which they might be entitled. So, for example, many claimants totally miss out on their entitlement to SB single payments and to additional requirements, such as those for heating.[24] The ability of the DHSS to check mistakes or fraudulent claims, whether intentional or otherwise, at an early stage, must also be hampered. As Roger Smith shows in Chapter 9, there has been a steady move away from the proper and due administration of claims towards a pattern of control on the basis of fear by a claimant that he or she will be selected for examination by the 'fraud squad'.

Statistics which purport to show improved efficiency therefore ring very hollow to staff and claimants alike. Efficiency is not just the number of cases handled, the numbers caught out in petty fraud and the money saved by cheeseparing in the payment of discretionary benefits. The quality and speed of service to the claimants, the adequacy of advice, the levels of take-up of benefit, the perceived fairness of the social security system overall and also the morale of staff should be measured in any true test of efficiency.

Priorities in the administration

The pressures on local offices have been compounded by government policy decisions on the priorities for available resources.

The most glaring example of this was the decision to introduce Specialist Claims Control (SCC) teams into the DHSS in 1980. As Roger Smith explains, this necessitated 1,050 extra staff, at a time when cuts throughout the rest of the DHSS were just getting under way. The details of SCC teams, the climate of harassment and intimidation they create, and the fact that their apparent savings are based on highly questionable accounting measures, are dealt with in Chapter 9. Here, let it be said that there can be little doubt that SCC teams have played a major role by diverting attention from the proper payment of benefit to the marginal activity of fraud and abuse. They must have deterred unknown thousands of genuine claimants.

SCC teams have led to a serious deterioration in staff relations with claimants in local offices. They also symbolise the government's attitude towards claimants, apparently based on the assumption that most claimants are likely to be 'scroungers'. A responsible approach would, instead, instruct the administration of the DHSS to give claimants the best possible service and ensure maximum take-up of benefits.

The introduction of postal claims forms, and the reduction in home visiting, are part of the same narrow approach. Measures introduced to cut the numbers of staff change the nature of the administration of SB by moving it away from even attempting to provide a humane and caring benefit service.

Local offices

The conflicting pressures of cuts in staff and resources, and the negative effect of current policies on the setting up of priorities, combined with a massive increase in the number dependent on means-tested benefits, when benefits themselves are under attack, all meet in one place: the DHSS local office.

It is understandable that claimants, who are bewildered by the complexity of the system, who face delays and difficulties, with long queues and a failure to make telephone contact, are hostile to staff. The staff themselves are both frustrated and under stress. Many have described the situation as being 'under siege'—and it is often the lowest paid and most junior staff who have to bear the brunt of the problem.

In inner-city offices, the increase in the number of SB claimants — and the proportion of those who are unemployed — is much higher than elsewhere. In Birmingham and Oxford in 1982 the pressures brought about by this situation led to strike action lasting four months. Many other offices have been involved in industrial action, often based on spontaneous walkouts. The DHSS trade unions' experience is that management's only response to these desperate situations is to seek overtime working, employ casual staff or draft in staff on a temporary basis from another office.[25]

Following the strike in Birmingham (covered in more detail in Chapter 4) and another in Oxford in 1982, management and unions embarked on a joint review of the 'complementing' system, whereby the number of staff necessary to run DHSS local offices is determined. The review concluded that 'the present complementing system does not adequately provide the correct number of staff to match workloads at all times'.[26] It came up with some proposals for improvements, but many of them will take several years to work their way through the system. Others need the Treasury to agree before extra staff will be made available.

Ultimately, all this hinges on the more fundamental issue of central government policies on civil service staffing. Unless the government agrees to make staffing fit the job to be done, and ensures that the aim is to get the job done properly, no complementing system will be able to resolve the crisis which is being caused by a desperate shortage of staff.

New technology: golden opportunity or next crisis?

The next big crisis in the DHSS is likely to arise with the introduction of new technology. New technology could provide a golden opportunity for major improvements in the administration of the social security system. It could release resources from boring and tedious jobs into areas such as benefit take-up and welfare provision. Computerised assistance could reduce pressure in local DHSS offices and improve the service to the public. Instead, there is every indication that the government is intent on squandering that opportunity. The Treasury insists that all new technology projects must be self-financing; the cost of the equipment must be met by staff savings.[27] This policy, on top of the already inadequate staffing levels, can only exacerbate the pressures on local office staff, and limit possible improvements in service to the public, in take-up of benefit and in welfare provision.

The DHSS's plans for computerisation over the next 20 years—known as the 'operational strategy' — include an estimated staff saving of 25,000 jobs.[28] The estimated total costs of the operational strategy are some £700m, with cumulative net savings in staff and administrative costs of some £1,200m.[29] Early in 1985 microcomputers are due to be introduced into each local office, as the first stage in this process, with an estimated saving of up to four staff in each local office as a result.

The civil service unions' policy towards new technology is to cooperate so long as there are no job losses. They consider that the benefits of new technology should be shared, claimants should be given a better service and staff should ultimately achieve a shorter working week. Without agreement on these points — and current government policies make agreement unlikely — there will be no union cooperation with any attempt to introduce new technology.

The DHSS does not have a very good track record on introducing new technology to local offices. As it admitted to the Public Accounts Committee,[30] between £6m and £12m of public funds were spent on its first attempt at local office computerisation under the 'Camelot' project, which had to be abandoned.

The DHSS's latest computer plans for investment in new technology are expected to cost £20m in the period 1985/86. The House of Commons Public Accounts Committee could not 'avoid expressing some unease about the viability of this stage of LOP [Local Office Project] and the continuing uncertainties in what is both an extremely expensive and uncertain series of computer developments'.[31]

The question of new technology is particularly important at the moment, given Norman Fowler's reviews. The Public Accounts Committee said mildly that it assumed the DHSS 'will also consider carefully the possible implications of the current fundamental review of social security benefits'.[32] Individual claimants, though, have a right to be rather more concerned.

The decision to press ahead with the system for introducing microcomputers into local offices, before the outcome of the social security reviews was known, means either that the DHSS has gambled £20m in the hope that the systems will fit in with the reviews, or that the reviews have been tailored to suit the plans for computerisation. Either outcome could be disastrous for claimants. It is clear that the introduction of new technology is not planned as a panacea for the current crisis in SB administration.

Conclusion: how can the crisis be resolved?

The crisis in administration has been brought about by the DHSS being expected to meet two conflicting demands: on the one hand, ministers are calling for savings on both benefits and staffing; on the other, increasing numbers of people are reliant on means-tested benefits. The government and the DHSS have responded by introducing procedural changes, such as the postal claims forms, by transferring responsibility for benefits and their administration elsewhere, as in the case of sick pay and housing benefit; by cutting the levels of benefits themselves; by limiting advertising and publicity as a means of keeping take-up depressed; by concentrating on fraud and thus deterring thousands of legitimate claims; and by introducing new technology, apparently another opportunity to make some savings. All this will do nothing to halt the serious deterioration in the standard of service that the DHSS offers; rather, it is motivated by the wish to save money and limit public expenditure.

The community has every right to expect a good level of service. It depends on the provision of adequate resources, backed up by a sufficiently staffed administration. It requires benefits to be set at adequate levels, and non-means-tested social insurance benefits adapted to cover the needs of contemporary society, so that the social assistance benefits — where the actual crisis lies — can revert to their safety-net role.[33]

The self-respect of DHSS staff, who are currently over-worked, under-paid, and given little cause for high morale, and of claimants, who currently get a poor service and are not encouraged or helped to claim their full entitlement, must be restored.

References

1 'From the cradle to the grave: social security for all the people', Society of Public Servants (SCPS) and Civil and Public Servants Association (CPSA) joint evidence to the social security reviews, 1984.

2 *House of Commons Hansard*, 22 December 1983, col 383W.

3 As note 2 above.

4 *House of Commons Hansard*, 19 November 1984, col 63W. The exact figures are 1 May 1979, DHSS staff 98,021½; 1 July 1984, DHSS staff 90,065½.

5 SCPS and CPSA documents.
6 SCPS claim for 10,000 extra staff in process of compilation.
7 *The Government's Expenditure Plans 1984-5 to 1986-7*, Cmnd 9143-II.
8 DHSS correspondence.
9 *House of Commons Hansard*, 31 July 1984, col 229W.
10 See note 7 above.
11 Greater London Citizens' Advice Bureaux, *No Benefit: problems people face claiming supplementary benefit*, 1984.
12 See note 7 above.
13 See note 7 above.
14 *Financial Times*, 6 November 1984.
15 Letter from Michael Meacher MP to Norman Fowler, *Financial Times*, 19 October 1984.
16 See note 9 above.
17 See Family Service Unit, *Social Insecurity: the administration of supplementary benefits*, Discussion Paper, 1984; Greater London Citizens' Advice Bureaux, see note 11 above; J Allbeson and R Smith, *We don't give clothing grants any more*, CPAG 1984; National Consumer Council, *Of Benefit to All: a consumer view of social security*, 1984; and the Policy Studies Institute's detailed Working Papers on the subject.
18 Family Service Unit, see note 17 above.
19 See note 11 above.
20 Allbeson and Smith, see note 17 above.
21 *The Director of the Regional Planning Organisations Report for the Review Year 1982-3, Priorities Annex*, DHSS 1983, p 39.
22 National Consumer Council, see note 17 above.
23 See note 22 above.
24 Disability Alliance, *Counting the Costs: a study of the take-up of supplementary benefit additional requirements*, 1983.
25 DHSS correspondence.
26 DHSS Management and Departmental Trade Union Side, 'Enquiry into the local office complementing system: report of the joint working party', 1984.
27 DHSS correspondence, and see note 9 above.
28 *Social Security Operational Strategy: a framework for the future*, DHSS 1982.
29 *House of Commons Hansard*, 6 December 1984, col 267W.
30 *Twenty-seventh Report from the House of Commons Public Accounts Committee 1983-4*.
31 See note 30 above.
32 See note 30 above.
33 See note 1 above.

4. Flat broke
the Birmingham strike
SUE WARD

As other chapters in this book have shown, the crisis within the Department of Health and Social Security (DHSS) is stretching many social security offices to the limit. Judy McKnight explains the background to this and the staff's response in Chapter 3. This chapter is a case study of the experience in one particular city, Birmingham, where the strains passed breaking point in September 1982, and staff started to walk out on strike. It took four months to settle the dispute, and a further five for all the social security offices to re-open.

Birmingham Welfare Rights Group, representing most of the city's advice and law centres, published a pamphlet, *Flat Broke*, written by Sally Coetzee,[1] about the strike in 1983. This chapter is a summary of that pamphlet, published by kind permission of Sally and the Group.

The background to the strike

Birmingham was once a by-word for working-class affluence. Now it is a symbol of national industrial decline. Unemployment in the city rose from 5.7 per cent in May 1979, slightly below the national average, to 16.2 per cent in May 1983, well above the national average and rising faster than almost anywhere in the country.[2]

The scale and speed of Birmingham's economic collapse put huge pressure on the DHSS's local offices as unemployed people turned to the welfare state for help. In one 12-month period alone (February 1981 — February 1982), an extra 27,702 people in Birmingham claimed supplementary benefit (SB).[3] At the same time, the number of staff was being held back owing to government spending restrictions. There was also a series of changes to benefit rules, which created a large volume of paperwork.

For the public, all this meant delays, expense and acute and unnecessary financial hardship at a time when people were already being forced to adjust to life on the dole. For the social security staff, it meant intolerable pressure at work, clashes with claimants and a growing awareness that sooner or later something was going to give. In the end, it was the social security system.

Throughout the summer of 1982, West Midlands County Council ran a vigorous campaign to highlight the economic crisis facing the region and, more specifically, the problems for claimants caused by the strains on the social security system. In June Terry Pitt, the county's senior economic adviser, reported that about 280,000 people in a region that was once the workshop of Britain were living on the poverty line, and that about 100,000 people in the county were not getting all the benefits they were owed by an increasingly remote welfare system. The report also pointed to an issue that was to become central in the dispute: the inadequate staffing levels in social security offices. Terry Pitt wrote:

> The stark change from the relative affluence a decade ago is felt by people for whom claiming is a new and often bewildering experience and by DHSS staff attempting to operate a complex system within a region which has never before had to gear itself up to deal with the effects of mass unemployment.
>
> At best this has led to a small increase in staff to deal with the massive increase in workload; at worst it has led to some reduction in staffing levels. The failure of staff levels to grow in line with the increase in workloads leads to a series of effects which ultimately reduce the quality of service claimants receive. The increasing pressure of work leads to a lowering of staff morale, higher absentee rates and a greater staff turnover.

The report sparked off an angry correspondence with the DHSS regional controller. But there was no response from social services secretary Norman Fowler. In October, after the strike had started, West Midlands county councillor Geoffrey Edge said:

> Almost four months later our warnings have been totally disregarded — the Secretary of State has taken absolutely no action other than to send us a derisory acknowledgment in the form of a standard civil service postcard. I would appeal to Norman Fowler to show some compassion for the poor in his own area, and to take immediate steps to rectify a situation which through his own neglect he has allowed to escalate.[4]

MPs' questions unanswered

Meanwhile, MPs from the region were meeting official obstruction in their attempts to highlight the growing problems. In a reply to one MP in February 1982,[5] Prime Minister Margaret Thatcher said that her government had been trying to introduce a simplified procedure and that staffing levels were reviewed so that they bore a direct relation to the increased load on local offices. 'There have been some difficulties due to bad weather and the rail strikes, and some letters and forms have not been received', she added.

Another MP asked about the number of SB claims and staff at the DHSS offices in Handsworth. Lynda Chalker, then parliamentary under-secretary, said that the number of people registered for welfare benefits there had increased from 18,160 to 20,362 over three years, while staff had decreased from 244 to 199 over the same period. But she then refused to give three other West Midlands MPs similar information on other offices on the grounds that:

> It is misleading simply to compare numbers of claims with numbers of staff at any particular time.
>
> Staffing levels are reviewed and adjusted frequently, under arrangements negotiated and agreed with the central departments and the trade unions. Staff resources also vary over time and local and regional managers are responsible for making adjustments within and between offices to cope in the most efficient and effective way with variations in workloads and staffing...
>
> For all these reasons it is not possible to make valid comparisons between one year and another. It is to be expected that some offices or sections should come under particular pressure from time to time, and this is the current situation in some offices in the West Midlands. Regional and local office managers are taking appropriate action.[6]

Trade union complaints ignored

As delays in the system grew longer, public tempers grew shorter, and there were several assaults on staff. Civil service unions repeatedly asked DHSS management to take action.

As far back as September 1981, the unions had forecast in a national report to the Public Accounts Committee that 'management would inevitably be faced with growing unrest among local staff and the prospect of recurring conflict'.[7] Throughout the winter of 1981 and the spring of 1982 the unions complained repeatedly about staff shortages in the Birmingham offices. Twice the disagreements were serious enough to be registered officially with the DHSS at regional level.[8]

Management finally agreed—on April Fool's day, ironically—to send an inspection team to the offices at Erdington and Handsworth. The team's report (which was not made publicly available) said that staff dealing with SB claims were overloaded with work, and there was a lack of proper monitoring and organisation.[9]

Statistics were inaccurate, too much effort was spent recouping small debts, and too much time was spent receiving people at the offices, as against dealing with their cases. An additional 30 staff, out of the region's reserve of 80 people, was allocated to the two offices, but this was not enough to have a major effect on the problems.

In May the unions decided to go public. The Society of Civil and Public Servants (SCPS) launched a campaign to warn councillors, MPs, press and public of the serious position in the DHSS. It singled out the government's inflexible attitude towards staffing levels and its drive for public spending cuts as the main culprits.

> Our concern is not only over the threat to jobs and the services offered to the public, but also over the apparently random, illogical, and politically motivated nature of these cuts...
>
> If this trend is not halted and reversed, the net result will be chaos — for managers, employees, and the public alike. Our members, who have shown a remarkable degree of application and loyalty to the public they serve, now believe that the time has come to say 'enough'.[10]

Rundown to September

Throughout the summer there were sporadic crises in DHSS offices in the city. At Erdington, in north Birmingham, staff holidays compounded by sick leave had led to a complete breakdown in the bureaucratic machine by mid-August. An emergency plan was drawn up, but within two weeks it had to be abandoned. Staff at the office invited Norman Fowler, as one of the local MPs, to visit the office and see the chaos. He never took up the offer. At the end of August another emergency plan was drawn up, concentrating all work on the most important cases. But it was too late to stop the approaching disaster.

In early September, when Richard Horton, a union official, visited the Erdington office, he found chaos: 'Drawer space had run out and case papers were piled high on desks and in cardboard boxes on the floor... There were virtually no staff to be seen: most were doing urgent counter work. Morale was depressingly low.'[11] The local manager estimated that 536 telephone queries had not been dealt with, 1,500 pieces of post were outstanding, and there were 300 claims for health benefits and 350 cases of overpayments which had to be chased up.[12] Two hundred and fifty claimants were coming in each day, a third of them asking about delays in payment of their benefits. In addition, 1,300 unemployed school-leavers would shortly be making their first claims—plans to use the three office trainees to handle this work were blocked by the unions.

On 15 September two of the three receptionists telephoned in sick. The third went to open the office up and found about 80 people lined up outside. She burst into tears. Three staff members were drafted in from other parts of the office to run the public counter, which left their three desks unattended. By 11.30am, 200 people had arrived at the office. At a hastily convened meeting of the two main unions, the office manager said he could not guarantee to provide extra staff for the next morning. So, at 2.00pm, union members voted five to one to strike. It was eight months before the office was re-opened to the public. During that time the entire benefits system came to an almost complete halt in the second largest city in the country.

The offices shut down

Workers at the Erdington office were convinced that the only long-term solution was an increase in permanent staff. So when, on 18 September, the DHSS regional management offered temporary help to clear the office, they rejected the offer and voted to stay out on strike.

The unions quickly declared the strike official, and made contact with MPs, who in turn met DHSS under-secretary Tony Newton in an attempt to get the government to respond to the strike. This failed, and over the next eight weeks all the other DHSS offices in the city shut down. On 28 September staff at the Northfield and Sparkhill offices joined in the dispute, followed, on 4 October, by those at Ravenhurst. The next day the DHSS wrote to two union officials claiming they had failed to provide 'evidence of inadequate staffing levels'. Staff at a fifth office, Washwood Heath, walked out on 7 October. By the time the Handsworth staff walked out on 13 October, it was clear that this would be a long-running dispute, and the government began intensive negotiations.

It was hoped that the national staff review, due out in October, would provide the basis for a compromise. However, under the criteria used, the review showed no serious lack of staff. Towards the end of October a new peace offer was heavily rejected by a mass meeting of strikers in Birmingham, and by 11 November all the offices were closed to the public. On 3 December 27,391 staff throughout the country staged a national stoppage in support of the strike.

As the social security offices shut down, emergency centres were set up in Erdington and Digbeth, and at Five Ways House in Birmingham, the DHSS's Midlands headquarters. In one of the ironies of the dispute, many of the staff who ran these centres were recruited from the DHSS's notorious Specialist Claims Control Unit — more commonly known as the fraud squad (see

Chapter 9). The centres made special flat-rate payments to people who would usually get SB. These included people who were making their first ever claim, such as newly widowed women or people whose unemployment benefit had run out. They also included some people whose ordinary order books were finished, as the skeleton staff left in some offices could not cope with providing replacements.

Conveniently—and perhaps not by coincidence—the government had brought in regulations on 9 August to allow emergency payments to be made on the SB budget, at a level left to the discretion of the Secretary of State.[13] Single people who did not have their own homes were paid £19 per week; and married couples and single parents were paid only £40 and £24 per week, respectively, regardless of the size of their families. There was no extra money for rent,[14] for children or for special heating or diet expenses incurred by the old and chronically ill. There were no single payments to help pay large one-off bills, like clothes for a new baby or furniture for a new home.[15] Many people had to rely on charity. In extreme cases, voluntary organisations and social workers gave furniture, clothes and sometimes even food to the people stranded by the welfare state. Travelling to the emergency centres meant long expensive journeys for many people, and for the frail and elderly these could be physically impossible.

The government was warned about the likely consequences of a strike which deprived so many people of their basic income. In the late autumn, the Chief Constable of the West Midlands was reported in the local press as saying that he hoped the strike would end quickly, as he feared what might happen. In the event, there was nothing for the authorities to fear. Perhaps people had been hammered too hard to fight back. Propped up by friends, relatives, voluntary organisations and emergency payments, they somehow scraped by. Their acquiescence may have passed for success as far as the emergency payments system was concerned. But it was clear from the people coming to the advice centres that they survived only with difficulty, humiliation, and real hardship. The flat rate emergency payments left them flat broke.

What happened to people during the strike[16]

Living standards for Shirley, Dave and their two daughters plummeted when Dave lost his job shortly after the strike started. The family was forced to live on £40 per week emergency money.

> Two or three days before the emergency payment comes we eat flour and water dumplings with cups of tea. Occasionally there may be enough potatoes for chips. Luckily, the children get school dinners...

> The children need shoes. They're still wearing trainers in the snow. Shirley has to wear slippers inside and outside the house. We had to borrow a skirt and blouse for Sally to go to school in. She gets upset because she can't join the cookery classes at school—we can't afford to provide the ingredients.
>
> Both the gas and electricity have threatened to disconnect.
>
> There's the constant stress of coping on a reduced income. Your family suffers because there is that tension hanging over you all the time... you're arguing with the wife because you feel so hopeless. The wife is arguing with you because she is wondering how on earth she can feed us all on such a small amount.

Single parents got even lower payments. One mother, a single parent with three children, aged 14, 9 and 7, said:

> We have not managed very well on the £24 a week emergency payments. Even shopping around for cheaper food, my children and I have had to cut down from three decent meals a day to just one. I could not cope with clothing, and I have been threatened with disconnection of my electricity as I have a £60 bill which I have no way of paying. I have not been able to pay any rent as this would leave me with only £1 a week for food. I have had to get credit from my local grocery shop, using my child benefit book as security...
>
> For three months my son has not been able to attend school because he has no suitable clothing or shoes. My daughter has had to go to hospital once a week. I have had to go to the same hospital due to a kidney infection. The hospital is some distance away, and although the bus fares were reimbursed, half the time I did not have the single fare to get there.
>
> For Christmas my children and I went to stay in a charity home. That was arranged by community workers, and if it wasn't for them my children would have had no Christmas at all. Since Christmas I have had nothing to cook on, and have had to depend on different neighbours to cook all my children's food.

Some people were able to get the backing of those with enough muscle to fend off the worst of their debts. It took the combined efforts of an advice centre, the assistant chief accountant of the Midlands Electricity Board, the personal social services section of the Birmingham Voluntary Services Council, a DHSS regional officer and a solicitor to get one woman and her two children the money they were owed.

For many people problems arose because the normal bureaucracy of life on social security came grinding to a halt. A cancer patient, left for weeks without money, and a newly widowed woman, forced to keep four children on £24 a week, were just two of the people who turned to members of the Welfare Rights Group for help. For some, order books which ran out could not be replaced. For others, what should have been happy events meant financial disaster — for example, the birth of a new baby threw a carefully balanced family budget into complete confusion because the benefits were not forthcoming.

What would be minor mishaps for people in work brought near destitution for claimants. An unemployed man whose wallet was stolen had to live for two weeks over Christmas on borrowed money because he could not get any response from the DHSS. A young couple had to wait months for a grant to buy furniture for their new home. They had not put curtains up at the window when they first moved in, so the postman delivering the cheque thought the house was empty and took it back to the post office. The next day the strike started. The couple were both in their teens, and the wife was eight months pregnant.

Throughout the strike the civil service unions stressed that their interest was in the standard and future of the social security service. But for people on social security, these arguments wore thin. It is hard to believe that something is for your own good when it turns a poor service into a non-existent one. The Claimants' Union had its own version of the dispute:

> The running of the emergency benefit offices was something of a sick joke... The Claimants' Union heard from a lot of people who had been refused an emergency payment because the person they saw decided not to give them one...
>
> The rhetoric about striking for our benefit remains just rhetoric. The unions say they have to face abuse from the claimants, but the social security system is itself an abuse to those who have to rely on it.[17]

At the end of the strike

At the beginning of January 1983, after almost four months without pay, the strikers voted at a mass meeting to accept a government peace package. This provided 45 extra staff for Birmingham offices on a temporary basis until the end of March, a study into the particular problems of inner-city offices and a more general review of the way that staffing levels in offices are calculated. Neither of the reports has been published. However, it is believed by the unions that they recommend that 90 extra staff be moved to Birmingham from other Midlands offices, and recognise that all big city offices face serious problems.

When the strikers went back to work on 17 January, they faced a huge task. Thousands of cases had to be transferred back from the emergency centres to the local offices. Thousands of benefits had to be upgraded or altered because of a whole string of rule changes during the strike. Arrears and overpayments had to be sorted out. Finally, the offices had to be re-opened to the public.

Industrial action over staffing continued. Only a few weeks after returning to work, staff at Sparkhill took action. Then staff at Erdington staged three one-day stoppages, followed by walk-outs at Handsworth, Northfield and South Yardley offices. All these stoppages were in protest against the use of overtime and casual staff. The unions wanted to make sure that there were enough permanent staff to run the service efficiently.

Delays in transferring cases back to the local social security offices left many people on emergency payments weeks after the strike was over. By the end of January only 2,250 out of a total of 24,500 cases had been transferred. Thirty-thousand cases had been classed as 'dormant' and 12,250 people were still on the emergency payroll. This created extra difficulties as other authorities assumed that, since the strike was over, people could now pay off their debts. A bedridden 81-year-old woman was sent a letter from the city council seeking possession of her council house because she had not paid the rent for several months. But the woman was still on emergency payments which were hardly enough to meet her immediate needs, let alone pay £21.50 a week rent. She was 'shattered' by the letter. The council claimed, however, that it was 'just a formal notice to inform the tenant that they owe us money and that, now the strike is over, it should be paid when people receive their backdated money from the DHSS. Some people have not been using this money to repay the debt and this letter serves as a reminder.'

The new housing benefit scheme, introduced during the strike, created further problems. (Nick Raynsford, in Chapter 5, describes how great were the difficulties caused by its introduction on a national scale.) It involved the DHSS transferring responsibility for the rent element of benefit to the council. Money was also owed from the DHSS to the housing authority for rent due before the change-over. At one stage, the DHSS owed Birmingham city council more than £1m in rent arrears on council houses.

Fuel boards also started increasing pressure on their customers. During the strike the boards' policy was not to prosecute people on social security for debts which they obviously could not pay. They also reduced weekly instalments for people on 'easy payment' schemes. But as soon as the strike had officially ended, the boards started recouping the large debts which had accumulated during the extremely cold winter. They assumed that people's income would automatically be restored to its normal level, and that they would immediately get their arrears of benefit.

Meanwhile, tension was again growing in the social security

offices. Arrears of work had not been cleared and big backlogs of new cases were building up. In addition, the new postal claim form, designed to cut down on interviews, was causing problems. It was too complicated, and in some offices 70 per cent were coming in incorrectly filled in and so needed to be sent back.[18]

By 18 March the position was once again serious enough for the unions to complain. This time, they asked for the re-opening of some of the offices to be delayed because of their 'grave concern' about the backlogs of work. Gradually, however, despite their protests, all the offices were re-opened to the public. The last, Erdington, only re-opened on 24 May, halfway through the general election campaign.

The government subsequently decided to study the 'lessons' of the DHSS dispute, including the apparent 'success' of the emergency payment system. Tony Newton, then a junior minister at the DHSS, told the *Birmingham Post:* 'I think we had expected to find more difficulties than seem to have occurred. We intend to find out why these anxieties did not fully materialise.'[19] The DHSS mounted a major study of people living on social security in Birmingham, interviewing 115 people who had received emergency benefit during March and April 1983, and 60 who had not. The questionnaire for the former was 65 pages long, with 94 questions. Apart from questions about when and where benefits were paid, it asked:

> Did you think the regular amount of payment you got sent was fair or not?
>
> Do you think there were any advantages in getting the emergency payments compared with normal supplementary benefit?
>
> During the time you were getting emergency payments, would you say you had to cut down on your heating or not?
>
> . . . did you have to cut down, or change the kind of food your family were eating while you were getting the emergency payments?
>
> . . . did you or your family have the use of any of these items, whether working or not: TV set, video tape recorder, fridge, deep freeze or fridge freezer, vacuum cleaner, washing machine, tumble dryer, dish washer, telephone?
>
> . . . about how often did you manage to go out to something that cost you money? For example, to a public house, club, to the cinema or football match or to play bingo?
>
> Did problems over money cause any stress or arguments in your family. . . Would you say these were just minor upsets, or were they really serious arguments?
>
> . . . was there a car or van normally available for use by you? Was that one or more than one?

Finally, if you had to claim emergency payments again, is there anything you would like to see done differently?

At least one person on emergency payments had very clear answers to these questions. In a letter to Jeff Rooker MP, a single mother wrote:

> No one can afford to pay the high council rents, the high bus fares, the ever increasing price of food. No one can afford to buy extra food, clothes, shoes or toys for their children this Christmas—not on £22 a week.

The results of the survey have not been published, and it may be that the DHSS does not consider its methodology sufficiently sound to stand up to publicity. Since then, the DHSS has carried out another survey of claimants in connection with the supplementary review. Among other questions, claimants were asked whether they *thought* they could live on a flat-rate benefit. The hypothetical responses should be compared with the real evidence of the hardship and difficulty experienced by claimants in Birmingham during the strike.

The lessons

Birmingham Welfare Rights Group, in a 'postscript' to *Flat Broke*, drew out the lessons they themselves learned. These included:

- Anyone with common sense will see that the social security system is not working. The four-month strike in Birmingham was just one outward sign of the turmoil inside the DHSS.
- Staffing levels in DHSS offices in Birmingham need radical reform as they are clearly inadequate. The unemployed, the sick and the elderly are paying the price in the form of delays and deficiencies in their benefits.
- The government may use false conclusions drawn from the strike to alter the social security system in a way that will devastate the living standards of the unemployed. In particular, the introduction of any flat-rate benefit seems likely to cause hardship, as it did in Birmingham.
- The secretary of state should fulfil his legal obligations by ensuring that all claimants get the state benefits to which they are entitled. The government's failure has forced many voluntary organisations to pick up the bills of the welfare state.
- What happened in Birmingham could happen elsewhere in the country. It is an indictment of the indifference of both government and DHSS management that social security staff and the public should face such chaos.

References

1 *Flat Broke: how the welfare state collapsed in Birmingham*, Birmingham Welfare Rights Group 1983.
2 'Family Income Trends: report of the senior economic adviser to the Economic Development Committee', West Midlands County Council, July 1983. The report quotes DHSS sources.
3 As note 2 above.
4 *Birmingham Evening Mail*, October 1982.
5 *House of Commons Hansard*, 4 February 1982, cols 197-8W.
6 *House of Commons Hansard*, 16 February 1982, cols 141-2.
7 SCPS/CPSA, Joint submission to Public Accounts Committee.
8 Handsworth and Erdington local offices registered disputes with the DHSS Midlands Region through CPSA.
9 Departmental inspection by the DHSS. Information eventually made available from non-attributable sources.
10 CPSA/SCPS press release, May 1982.
11 Internal report of Regional CPSA, issued to the DHSS, MPs and the press, September 1982.
12 As note 11 above.
13 Supplementary Benefit Amended (Determination of Questions) Regulations 1982, 7A(1).
14 Housing benefit was introduced during the course of the strike in a two-stage process in November 1982 and April 1983. At the beginning of the strike, therefore, claimants were being paid benefit by the DHSS to cover their rent and rates. Page 49 describes the problem caused by the delayed change-over to housing benefit after the strike was settled.
15 For claimants in normal circumstances, SB regulations allow 'single payments' in such cases. See J Allbeson and J Douglas, *National Welfare Benefits Handbook*, CPAG 1984, for details.
16 The evidence in this section is drawn from interviews with people conducted by members of Birmingham Welfare Rights Group involved in advice-giving, and from local newspaper stories.
17 Report of Handsworth (Birmingham) Claimants' Union to Birmingham Welfare Rights Group, April 1983.
18 Birmingham CPSA estimate of success rate during the first two months of the new postal claim form B1.
19 *Birmingham Post*, 24 February 1983.

5. The false hopes and fiasco: **housing benefit**

NICK RAYNSFORD

Chapter 1 pointed to the fact that housing benefit (HB), one of the major benefits now within the budget of the Department of Health and Social Security (DHSS) (although administered by local authorities), has had to bear the brunt of decisions in other areas of housing policy. This chapter looks at the introduction of HB in 1982-3 — an introduction which must be counted as one of the great wasted opportunities in the history of the welfare state. To see why the reform has turned out to be quite so disastrous, however, it is first necessary to look a little at its background.

The long history of failed reform

The whole range of housing subsidies and means-tested benefits was widely recognised in the 1970s to be inefficient and inequitable, as well as very expensive. It was graphically described as 'a dog's breakfast' by Anthony Crosland,[1] then Secretary of State for the Environment, who set up a review of the whole subject in 1975 as a prelude to reform.

In the first place, there was the series of tax exemptions and reliefs available to home-owners: tax relief on interest payments on mortgages up to a maximum value of £25,000 (raised to £30,000 in 1983), exemption from capital gains tax on the disposal of a home, and exemption from tax on the imputed rental income from the home (the former Schedule A tax). These benefits, available irrespective of means, give the largest benefit to those on high incomes occupying expensive accommodation, and are very costly. Mortgage interest tax relief alone cost £2.8 billion in 1983/84,[2] and the total cost of tax relief and exemptions on owner-occupied homes has been estimated at almost £5.5 billion in 1982/83.[3]

Second, there were general subsidies to council housing, from both central government and local rate fund contributions. These made possible the public sector house building and slum clearance programme of the inter-war and post-war period, for without them the costs of council housing would have been beyond the means of most of the people for whom it was being built. However, by the 1970s it was recognised that the distribution of these subsidies was not always rational or effective. They were not necessarily targeted to concentrate assistance in areas with high costs or large unmet housing needs, and they applied across the whole public housing stock, irrespective of the means of the tenants. They were also expensive, costing £2.2 billion in 1979/80.[4] Subsequently, though, they have been drastically reduced as a result of deliberate government cuts since 1979—by 1983/84 exchequer and rate fund contributions to council housing were only £629m.[5]

The government defended its cuts in general subsidies to council housing, and hence the substantial increases in rent levels, by saying that those tenants who could not afford to pay more would be protected by the third range of subsidies — the means-tested benefits. These were divided between housing additions for supplementary benefit (SB) recipients, administered prior to 1983 by the DHSS, and rent rebates and allowances and rate rebates, administered by local authorities.

The local authority system had grown up in a largely haphazard way, as individual councils introduced rebates or differential rent schemes from the 1930s onwards, but they were brought together into a national framework in the 1960s (for rates) and in the early 1970s (for rent). The assessment of benefit under the rebates and allowances scheme was, however, based on different principles from those used by the DHSS to assess the entitlement of SB recipients, and consequently, there was room for confusion and inequity. Many recipients were unaware of whether they would be better off claiming SB or rebates (the 'better-off' problem) — it was estimated in 1979 that 400,000 households were worse off than they need have been through choosing the wrong benefit.[6]

Take-up was also lower than it should have been—for example, in 1982 it was estimated that only 62 per cent of all households and only 33 per cent of families with children in private rented housing entitled to a rent allowance were actually receiving one (see Chapter 8).[7] The withdrawal of benefit as a recipient's income rose could also aggravate the 'poverty trap'. People caught in this poverty trap can find that an increase in gross income (such as a wage rise) may result in their being little or no better off—or even, in extreme cases, worse off. They have to pay more in tax and national insurance contributions and, at the same time, their means-tested benefits may be reduced or withdrawn entirely. A common criticism of the workings of the poverty trap is that they may discourage the low paid from doing overtime or looking for a better paid job—the 'disincentive' effect. Moreover, it seems grossly unfair to the low paid that the government can simultaneously urge them to work 'harder' and to claim means-tested benefits, when the combined effect may be to continue to trap them in poverty.

So, although rent rebates (for council tenants), rent allowances (for private tenants) and rate rebates (for tenants and home-owners) were targeted on those with low incomes, they suffered from two of the key problems of means-tested benefits — poor take-up and the potential creation of a poverty trap. (Table 1 shows the total cost of means-tested housing benefits in mid-1981.)

Table 1: *Means-tested housing benefits mid-1981*

	No of households (million)	*Annual cost (£m)*
SB housing additions (rent and rates)	2.9	1,670
Rent rebate	1.6	570
Rent allowance	0.2	60
Rate rebate	3.5	338
Total cost		*2,638*

Source: S Goss and S Lansley, What Price Housing?, SHAC 1984, p 13.

Sadly, Anthony Crosland's attempt to rationalise and reform the whole jumble of subsidies, including mortgage tax relief, failed to get off the ground. The review was not complete when he was moved from the Department of the Environment in 1976, and his successor, Peter Shore, showed no appetite for any radical reform of the system. The review, when finally completed in 1977, offered no more than a rationalisation of the status quo on the grounds that:

> Radical changes in long established financial arrangements are never easy. They are bound to cause problems for households who have planned their finances on the expectation that the current arrangements would continue. The question is whether the benefits of radical alternatives would sufficiently outweigh the advantages of the current forms of general assistance to justify the disruption that might be caused no matter how the new arrangements were introduced.[8]

The introduction of the scheme

With the door closed on a fundamental reform of housing subsidies, the idea of a more limited reform of the means-tested benefits began to be mooted. David Donnison, then Chairperson of the Supplementary Benefits Commission, was the principal advocate of what became known as a 'unified housing benefit':

> What we need is a single scheme of housing benefit which would cover all low income householders, whether or not they are

eligible for supplementary benefit. Such a scheme would replace rate rebates, rent rebates and allowances and the rent element of supplementary benefit, and, ideally, would extend to the owner occupier the help now given to the tenant through his rent rebate or allowance. It would need to meet 100 per cent of reasonable housing costs for all supplementary benefit claimants and should do the same for others, including people in full time work, on comparable incomes. The new benefit would then taper off as incomes rise above these levels.[9]

But while the case for such a scheme was being made, principally on the grounds of creating a fairer, simpler scheme which would eliminate the 'better-off' problem and be easier for claimants to understand, there were others who had different goals. The DHSS had already given an indication in *Social Assistance*, its review of the SB scheme, that: 'If the element of housing costs could be removed from the supplementary benefit scheme, it would . . . greatly simplify the task of DHSS and enable them to make substantial staff savings [of the order of 2,900].'[10] This possibility took on greater significance with the change of government in 1979. David Donnison has described his discussions with Patrick Jenkin, the new secretary of state at the DHSS:

> the government was determined to reduce the number of civil servants, and before long Patrick Jenkin was giving private assurances that he would achieve that. The only way DHSS could cut itself on a considerable scale in supplementary benefits—the most labour costly part of its services—was by getting rent payments out of the scheme.[11]

But while the DHSS was showing increasing enthusiasm for the idea of a unified HB, which would take housing costs out of SB, the Department of the Environment (DoE) was not so impressed. The scheme held no obvious advantages for it; on the contrary, the DoE would have the task of seeing that local authorities took on the administration of HB for SB recipients, as well as for rent rebate, rent allowance and rate rebate recipients, at the very time when it was pressing local authorities to reduce expenditure and staffing levels. The DoE's caution, proved by subsequent events to have been entirely justified, was clear from the tone of the consultation paper which first made public the proposals which were to result in the new HB scheme. After describing the framework of the proposals in *Assistance with housing costs*, a consultation paper issued by the DoE and the Welsh Office (*not* the DHSS), the government said it 'believes that this could form the basis of a workable reform but has by no means made up its mind'.[12]

The consultation paper and the events which followed its publication reveal the changing balance of motives leading up to the introduction of HB. The paper itself set out a series of explicit objectives.[13] These included many of the original aims, which commanded widespread support — to make the scheme easier to understand, so that claimants would be more likely to get their proper entitlement, to achieve greater fairness between different categories of claimants and to streamline the administration. However, two other key objectives — to introduce the scheme at no extra cost in benefit and to reduce the task imposed on public sector manpower as a whole — gave a clear indication of what was becoming the dominant objective.

Both of these further objectives had far-reaching implications. The first — the 'no extra cost' constraint — effectively undermined most of the original objectives for achieving a properly unified HB. For if the two separate systems — SB and rebates — were to be harmonised and brought into a workable unified system, this would inevitably require some additional expenditure to 'buy out' the anomalies and inconsistencies in the treatment of claimants. Indeed, David Donnison had explicitly warned in 1979 that 'the new benefit could not be introduced in a politically tolerable way without some increase in public expenditure — a very small one in relation to the money we are already spending on rent subsidy schemes for the poor, but a significant sum nevertheless'.[14] Although the consultation paper, and subsequent ministerial comments, implied that the scheme would achieve the original objectives, it can be no coincidence that it was now referred to simply as the HB scheme — the 'unified' had been dropped.

Instead of simplifying the old arrangements, the new proposals introduced a whole new series of complexities, including differential tapers for pensioner and non-pensioner households, and the 'topping-up' scheme known as HB supplement. These were necessary to avoid making a number of former SB recipients worse off (in some cases, by substantial sums) as a result of being reassessed under the 'rebates' formulae. Thus, the 'no extra cost' constraint, and the consequent failure to achieve a unified HB framework, created even more complexities and anomalies than the schemes it replaced.

In addition to the original idealistic objectives, and the increasingly important financial and manpower objectives stated in the consultation paper, there was a third group of objectives, which can only be described as 'sops'. In the first place, the government, aware that the 'no extra cost' constraint inevitably meant cuts in benefit for some, stated that one objective was to minimise losses caused to individuals. Second, conscious that devolving responsibility for the new scheme fully to local authorities could result in widespread regional variations in the treatment of claimants, the consultation paper stated that the scheme should be uniform throughout Great Britain. Finally, to allay their natural anxieties about extra administration costs, a pledge was given, and repeated frequently by ministers, that all net additional costs incurred by local authorities as a result of taking on the new scheme would be reimbursed. All of these sops were, to a greater or lesser degree, incapable of being satisfied because of other constraints.

The 'no extra cost' constraint meant that the scheme, as devised, would make a very large number of people worse off. The government's original estimate—of 2,150,000 households (one in 10 of the population)—was soon seen to be an underestimate of the true extent of the losses. Safeguards introduced during the parliamentary debates on the scheme were only transitional—*deferring*, but not eliminating, some of the losses caused to some claimants by the new arrangements. And they also added further complexities.

The promise of a uniform scheme throughout Great Britain was quite unrealistic, without any national appeal machinery whose decisions would be binding on all authorities. Instead, the interpretation of the scheme's regulations is left to each individual authority, and the appeal machinery, which was finally conceded during the parliamentary debates,[15] operates separately within each authority's area, with no attempt at building up a body of precedents centrally.

The pledge that all additional local authority expenditure would be reimbursed was based on fundamentally unsound assumptions, the most basic of which was that local authorities would require fewer staff to operate the new arrangements than the DHSS would be shedding. The figures quoted at the time assumed a reduction of around 2,300 DHSS staff, with local authorities needing to employ in total between 1,500 and 1,600 new staff.[16] It is now conceded by ministers that local authorities have had to employ more staff than the 2,400 which the DHSS has now claimed to have 'saved'.[17] The unrealistic assumptions about the number of staff required have had dire consequences. There was a totally inadequate provision of £5m (averaging around £12,000 per authority) for 'setting up' costs in 1982/83,[18] the year in which all the preparation, computer programming and staff training ought to have taken place if the scheme was to operate properly. Local estimates of the number of cases likely to be transferred from the DHSS to the authority were also frequently found to have gravely underestimated the workload.[19] All this contributed to the inadequate preparation and staffing levels which, in turn, led to the chaos surrounding the introduction of HB.

The inherent contradictions of the objectives spelt out in the consultation paper were clear to those working in the field from the very beginning. Indeed, the defects of the scheme outlined in

Assistance with housing costs, and the potential problems which its implementation would bring, were already being documented in considerable detail in the summer of 1981 in some of the responses to the consultation paper.[20] Even so, the responses were not, as one might have expected, universally hostile. Voluntary organisations and pressure groups were generally critical, many calling for a complete rethink of the proposals. But the local authority associations, in the words of perhaps the best informed of their staff, 'gave a cautious welcome' to the proposals.[21]

What can explain this gross miscalculation? Two reasons stand out. First, like some other commentators and official bodies such as the Advisory Committee on Rent Rebates and Rent Allowances, the associations were probably unduly influenced by the original prospectus for the scheme. They believed that the proposals would, in fact, largely achieve the goals which David Donnison had advocated in the late 1970s — initially Donnison himself gave qualified support to the new proposals.[22] Second, and more important, many local authorities, and hence their associations, were seduced by the idea of reduced rent arrears resulting from all SB recipients having their rent, in effect, paid directly by the HB scheme. This prospect blinded many local authority representatives to the real implications for them of the government's proposed scheme. Ironically, reductions in arrears because of the 'rent direct' elements have not materialised to anything like the expected extent.[23]

But even if the local authority response to the scheme was cautiously supportive, the DoE remained unenthusiastic, and had it alone been responsible, it is doubtful if the fiasco would have taken place. The only explanation for the fact that this fundamentally flawed scheme was implemented would seem to be that the DHSS was determined to press ahead regardless. If this is the case, the DHSS was not acting from a proper concern to achieve the best possible scheme for claimants and administrators. If that had been the primary concern, time would have been allowed for reconsideration of some of the most obvious weaknesses, if not the whole scheme.

Instead, it appears that the DHSS chose to take over responsibility for the scheme from the reluctant DoE, and to rush it through in the fastest possible timetable, introducing legislation in December 1981 to allow for implementation of the scheme from November 1982. This reckless haste was surely a result of the DHSS's overriding concern to make savings through reducing manpower within the 1982/83 financial year. (Chapter 3 illustrates the importance that such a consideration has within the government.) Housing benefit allowed it to do this if it could be introduced in time. Hence, the rush to legislate, the failure to pause to read the

warning signs, and the unilateral DHSS action, rather than a joint approach with the DoE. It was a major and complex social policy change, implemented in an inherently unsatisfactory way, to an unrealistically tight timetable, for fundamentally the wrong reasons — a deplorable example of how not to do it. From this point on, a disaster was inevitable.

The scheme itself

The disaster which followed the full start of the scheme in April 1983 has been well documented.[24] Throughout Great Britain, hundreds of thousands of claimants experienced delays of weeks, months and, in some cases, more than a year before their benefit entitlement was assessed under the new system. This, despite the requirement in the regulations that determinations of benefit should be made, where practicable, within 14 days.[25] For many claimants, the delay caused serious hardship, and in some cases led to evictions. Communications were chaotic in many areas, with claimants being told one thing by DHSS offices and another by the local authority. In many areas, authorities were simply unable to cope with the volume of queries from claimants who had received no benefit or who were unsure if their benefit had been correctly assessed. Many authorities closed their doors to the public for some days or part days to enable the staff to work on the backlog of assessments rather than answer queries. In one authority, queues used to form outside the HB office hours before it opened because it became known that only the first 50 claimants would be seen — at a time when the backlog of assessments was over 7,000.[26] In many areas, breakdowns in the flow of paper between DHSS, local authority and claimant — particularly in the case of private tenants and HB supplement claimants — caused serious delays and non-payment of benefit.

Almost everywhere, there were reports of problems with the computer systems, which had generally been prepared at short notice. In most instances, they were inadequate, whether they were systems programmed 'in house' by local authorities, or those supplied by computer firms and software agencies. In some areas, the programmes were so unreliable and generated so many incorrect assessments that authorities reverted to manual assessments.[27] There were also considerable delays in delivery of software packages.

The initial DHSS response in the spring of 1983 was to play down the problems, ascribing the difficulties to 'teething troubles', and to express hopes that all would settle down soon. This stance was still being adopted in July 1983 when the problems, far from settling down, were as widespread and chronic as ever—illustrating how poorly informed the DHSS was of the actual situation.[28] DHSS ministers initially claimed that only 15 authorities were encountering difficulties;[29] but even a hastily revised figure of around one in five (ie, about 100) grossly underestimated the size of the problem. In contrast, many local authorities, not normally renowned for outspoken public criticism of the government, were quite explicit about what was happening. The Director of Finance in the London Borough of Bromley wrote on 15 June to Bromley claimants: 'Many of you will be aware that the new housing benefit system is a mess.'

As the evidence of the problems mounted, so did public criticism of the DHSS. The press was almost unanimous in its condemnation of the scheme, particularly after the government had compounded the earlier blunders by imposing a harsh and arbitrary £230m cut in HB in November 1983. The *Guardian*, as early as August 1983, commented: 'The scale of the housing benefit debacle must leave even the most cynical chronicler of bungling bureaucracy breathless with disbelief. It is quite simply the worst example of administrative chaos to have befallen the welfare state.'[30] A few months later, in the midst of the furore over the November package of cuts, *The Times* described HB as 'A bungled reform', and went on to attribute the problems to: 'the government's determination to foist on councils a welfare responsibility without ensuring that the administrative ground was well prepared. It was an attractive but misguided attempt to bring about major reform of social security at zero cost.'[31] The *Daily Telegraph* was equally critical, and contrasted the treatment of HB recipients with those receiving tax relief on mortgage payments: 'It hardly seems equitable to cut welfare spending on the relatively poor in the name of good housekeeping and then reward owner-occupiers with large subsidies...'[32]

The government's own back-benchers were also increasingly outspoken in their criticisms, one going so far as to describe HB as 'this act of gross social and political folly'.[33] Yet, it should have come as no surprise. The fiasco was entirely predictable, and had been predicted.[34] The reasons are clear cut. Three stand out.

First, as has been shown, with the unrealistic 'no extra cost' constraint making a unified and simplified scheme impossible, the scheme is inherently defective. It is riddled with complexities and anomalies, which cause acute difficulties for claimants and administrators alike, most of which are the inevitable result of the failure to unify the two former schemes, SB and rebates. Housing benefit supplement is the obvious example. There are several instances of double standards, where different rules apply to 'standard' as against 'certificated' claimants (the former on rebates, the latter on SB). Perhaps the most blatant of these is the recovery of overpayments, where strict rules supposedly apply in 'certificated' cases, but a very wide discretion is given to authorities in 'standard' cases.[35] For 'certificated' cases, there is a duty to make interim payments if the authority cannot complete the benefit assessment within 14 days, but no such obligation applies to 'standard' cases.[36] Significantly, these double standards do not occur in Northern Ireland, where the DHSS had to make improvements to the scheme after strong criticism from the Northern Ireland Assembly, which otherwise would not have supported the implementation of HB.[37] (The scheme initially applied only in England, Wales and Scotland.) This demonstrates how, for all the scheme's structural defects, some of its weaknesses could have been remedied had the DHSS allowed sufficient time before implementation *and* if the local authority associations in Britain had taken a tougher stand on the scheme when it was being first discussed. As it was, only the Conference of Scottish Local Authorities stood out against the proposals at that time.

Secondly, the rushed implementation of the scheme severely aggravated the problems. The regulations setting out the detailed provisions of the scheme were not available when the Bill introducing HB was before parliament. They were published only in summer 1982, giving local authorities a mere four months before implementation of the first stage of the scheme. This timetable was totally inadequate. Some authorities made matters worse by slow and inefficient administration, but the blame must lie squarely with the DHSS for imposing such an unrealistic timetable in the first place.

The DHSS itself became a victim of this pressure, for, without adequate time to sort out problems and anomalies, it had to send out a stream of amending regulations in the autumn and winter of 1982 and the spring of 1983—the final implementation date was postponed twice. Not surprisingly, this spate of last-minute amendments created further problems for local authority administrators and computer programmers. Yet the DHSS did not learn lessons from the débacle which ensued, for 12 months later it again rushed into effect a whole series of amendments to the scheme, together with major cuts in benefit, within an equally tight timetable. The 28 amending regulations and benefit cuts were approved by parliament only on 14 February 1984, with implementation due on 1 April.

Thirdly, the two government departments primarily involved in the scheme failed to work effectively together—a crucially important factor, but one that has received less attention than the other two. The DHSS's decision to proceed with the reform on its own meant that it lacked any practical experience of the potential problems of implementing a national scheme via about 500 individual local authorities. DHSS officials seem to have acted as though the local authorities were, in effect, no different from DHSS local offices — simply there to do what they were told by headquarters. Meetings with the local authority associations and the involvement of a few local authority staff in the standing committees was apparently considered all the consultation that was necessary. When the scale of the disaster was at last beginning to sink in at DHSS head office, officials adopted a tone of injured innocence, protesting that they had not been aware that the local authority associations would be unable 'to deliver their members'. Ministers compounded matters by trying to blame local authorities for what had gone wrong.[38]

The failure to provide any assistance in the complex computer programming requirements for the new scheme reflected how far the DHSS, still reliant on manual processing in its local offices, was out of touch with local authority practice. Publicity arrangements were also inadequate — the single leaflet prepared by the DHSS compared very unfavourably with the old 'There's money off rent' leaflets which the DoE had produced prior to HB.

Thus, DHSS officials were out of touch with what was actually going on in the local authorities. They also soon showed a surprising indifference to those claimants who had previously been the responsibility of the DoE (ie, the 3.9 million households receiving rent rebates and allowances and rate rebates). The shackling together of the two schemes had been done in a way which left marked anomalies. Almost all of these worked to the disadvantage of rebate as against SB recipients. The ex-rebate claimants not only had no entitlement to interim payments and no limitation on recovery of overpayments; they also suffered all the losses attributable to changed 'non-dependant deductions' and 'tapers'. Then, only four months after the full implementation of the scheme, a whole series of further cuts was pushed through by the DHSS, overwhelmingly loaded on to the same people. The weekly losses involved could be massive — £4.52 for a single pensioner with an income of £77, and £8 for a family with two children with the head of household earning £135.[39] On top of the losses, there was an intensified 'poverty trap' for those in low-paid work (see p 54). As MPs of all parties began to express concern and alarm at the full effects of the scheme, it became clear that ministers and the Cabinet did not have a working knowledge of its complexities.

The 3.9 million households who had been receiving rebates and allowances before the change-over had not been the responsibility of the DHSS in the past, and had been taken on only because HB provided it with opportunities for staff saving economies. Now, these households provided a convenient milch-cow from whom money could be extracted to satisfy the Treasury's demand for cuts. An added advantage was that it would be the local authorities, not the DHSS, who would be blamed by the victims of those cuts. The DoE compounded this by remaining silent. It had justified massive cuts in general housing subsidies (and consequent rent increases) on the grounds that rebates and allowances protected those on lower incomes; yet it raised no protest when the DHSS chose to savage the rebate and allowance scheme.

Against this background, it was hardly surprising that the November 1983 cuts package finally blew the lid off the HB cauldron. There was almost unanimous press condemnation of the cuts and of the chaotic implementation of the scheme,[40] and widespread back-bench dissatisfaction even threatened the possibility of a government defeat in the House of Commons. As a result, the government finally made two concessions.[41] The first was a cosmetic adjustment to the package of cuts.[42] In effect, it deferred some of the elements in the package until November 1984 or April 1985, reducing the 1984/85 saving to £185m, but nevertheless achieving almost all the planned savings in the subsequent year.[43]

The second concession, the promise of an independent review of the HB scheme, could have more significance.[44] However, it may prove equally cosmetic. As Fran Bennett shows in Chapter 10, the very restricted scope of the review holds out little hope that it will chart the way towards the radical restructuring of the whole system of housing subsidies which is so clearly needed.

Conclusion

Despite the tight timetable for the submission of evidence to the reviews, the quantity and quality of the responses was impressive.[45] Their message can be summarised as follows:

- The terms of reference for the review were unrealistically narrow; they should have included other related subsidies such as mortgage interest tax relief.
- The HB scheme is not, as has been suggested by ministers, over-generous; nor does it go too far up the income scale. On the contrary, people paying average rents cease to be entitled at surprisingly low income levels. At 1983/84 rates, £132 per week was the maximum qualifying income for a married couple with two dependent children paying the average local authority rent.[46] There is no case—indeed, no scope—for further benefit cuts.
- The structure of the HB scheme is fatally flawed by its failure to unify the two preceding schemes. Tinkering with the existing schemes will not result in a proper solution, though some of the more absurd anomalies and problems may be ironed out.
- A radical new approach is necessary. In the long term, this

could be based on a universal non-means-tested allowance scheme, integrated with the tax system. Meanwhile, properly unified means-tested benefit, such as the single taper scheme proposed by SHAC (Shelter Housing Aid Centre),[47] would be a considerable improvement.

The case for a comprehensive and radical reform is overwhelming.

References

1 Quoted in Bernard Kilroy, *Housing Finance—Organic Reform?*, LEFTA (now Labour Finance and Industry Group) 1982, p 5.
2 *House of Commons Hansard*, 10 April 1984, col 82W.
3 Matthew Warburton, *Housing finance: the case for reform*, Catholic Housing Aid Society, Occasional Paper No 8, 1983, p 43.
4 Sue Goss and Stewart Lansley, *What Price Housing?*, 3rd ed, SHAC 1984, p 8.
5 As note 4.
6 David Donnison, 'Housing the poorest people', in *Housing Review*, May-June 1979, p 67.
7 *House of Commons Hansard*, 6 March 1984, cols 565-6W.
8 *Housing Policy: a consultative document*, Cmnd 6851, HMSO 1977, p 31.
9 See note 6 above, p 67.
10 *Social Assistance: a review of the supplementary benefit scheme in Great Britain*, DHSS 1978, p 58.
11 David Donnison, *The Politics of Poverty*, Martin Robertson 1982, p 191.
12 *Assistance with housing costs*, DoE/Welsh Office 1981, p 4.
13 As note 12, pp 2-3.
14 David Donnison, see note 6 above.
15 *House of Commons Official Report, Social Security and Housing Benefits Bill*, Standing Committee B, Seventeenth Sitting, 23 February 1982, col 561.
16 *DHSS: Housing Benefits Scheme, Report by Comptroller and Auditor General*, National Audit Office, October 1984, para 3.12.
17 *House of Commons Hansard*, 25 June 1984, col 312W. In November (*House of Commons Hansard*, 27 November 1984, col 472), it was conceded that at least 3,500 extra staff had been employed.
18 Housing Benefits Circular, HB (82)1, DHSS May 1982, para 41, p 10.
19 See, for example, Report of CIPFA Survey of 404 housing authorities in England and Wales, reported in *Local Government Chronicle*, 9 December 1983; Michael Hill, *Housing Benefit Implementation: from unified ideal to complex reality*, School for Advanced Urban Studies Working Paper 36, SAUS 1983, p 29.
20 See Nick Raynsford, 'For whose benefit?', *New Society*, 6 August 1981.
21 Steve Willcox, 'Housing benefit: the local authority view', *Poverty 53*, December 1982, CPAG, p 24.
22 See report of a speech by David Donnison to the Institute of Housing Conference, June 1981, in *Housing*, vol 17, no 9, September 1981.
23 See '£111m rent arrears for London', *London Housing*, December 1984, p 1.
24 For example, see Nick Raynsford, 'Backhanded benefit', *Roof*, July/August 1983; Michael Hill, see note 18 above; National Association of Citizens' Advice Bureaux, *Housing Benefit: the cost to the claimant*, 1984; Nick Fielding, 'The housing benefit fiasco', *Roof*, November/December 1983; Nicholas Timmins and David Walker, 'Anatomy of a bureaucratic

bungle', *The Times*, 20 January 1983; Stuart Weir, 'Housing nightmare', *New Society*, 26 January 1984; Barry Clark, Jane Daly, John Douglas, *Nobody's Benefit: a survey of the housing benefit scheme*, CPAG, July 1984; and Peter Kemp, *The Cost of Chaos*, SHAC, October 1984.

25 Reg 28.(5), SI 1982, no 1124.

26 See Stuart Weir, 'The poverty queue', *New Society*, 19 January 1984.

27 Clark, Daly and Douglas, note 24 above, Table 4; and Kemp, note 24 above, Table 2.1.

28 See, for example, *House of Commons Hansard*, 25 June 1984, col 312W; DHSS press release 83/165, 30 August 1983, and *Guardian*, 10 August 1983.

29 *House of Commons Hansard*, 28 June 1983, col 446.

30 *Guardian*, Editorial, 11 August 1983.

31 *The Times*, Editorial, 6 January 1984.

32 *Daily Telegraph*, Editorial, 20 January 1984.

33 Jerry Hayes MP, *House of Commons Hansard*, 14 February 1984, col 153.

34 See, for example, Nick Raynsford, note 20 above.

35 Regs 41 and 42, SI 1982, no 1124.

36 Reg 35, SI 1982, no 1124.

37 Northern Ireland Assembly, *Report on proposal for a draft housing benefits (Northern Ireland) Order*, NIA 51, HMSO, May 1983.

38 Dr Rhodes Boyson, BBC2 'Newsnight', 10 August 1983; DHSS press release 83/165, 30 August 1983.

39 *The Times*, 23 November 1983 (based on SHAC briefing paper, *The latest cuts*, November 1983).

40 *Guardian*, 8 August 1983; see also *Local Government Chronicle*, 12 August 1983, and *The Times*, 12 August 1983.

41 *House of Commons Hansard*, 6 February 1984, cols 612-14.

42 *House of Commons Hansard*, 6 February 1984, col 613.

43 *House of Commons Hansard*, 6 February 1984, cols 612-13.

44 As note 44 above.

45 See, for example, AMA, *Local Authorities and the Social Security System: evidence to the review bodies*, July 1984, para 10; *Submission by COSLA to the Housing Benefit Review*, July 1984, para 1.3; *Evidence to the Housing Benefit Review from CPAG*, July 1984, Introduction.

46 *Housing Benefit: the way forward*, SHAC 1984, pp 10-11.

47 See Peter Kemp and Nick Raynsford (eds), *Housing Benefit: the evidence*, Housing Centre Trust 1984.

6. The end of the line: **boarders and single homeless people**

RICK MIDDLETON

Beveridge's plans for the welfare state were based on a population made up of family units, living in decent housing, with almost all adult males in work — three assumptions that, by and large, have moulded the development and implementation of social security and other welfare policies. This chapter concerns some of those people for whom two, and often even three, of these assumptions do not hold: Department of Environment (DoE) figures for the late 1970s showed that unemployment among homeless single people was four times the rate as for those same people when they had a home.[1]

The main social security benefits—national insurance or basic supplementary benefit (SB)—are not designed to meet the needs of 'boarders' and single homeless people. Consequently, a variety of ad hoc alterations have been made from time to time to the core system in an attempt to 'cope' with them. Homeless families have also had severe problems (and continue to do so) for many of the same reasons. This chapter, however, concentrates on those without families.

A close study of this small area of the social security system reveals a great deal about the current crisis within and throughout the Department of Health and Social Security (DHSS). The day-to-day experience of those in groups working with homeless people gives the overwhelming impression that at ministerial level there is indifference and prejudice, whilst among the well-meaning policy-making civil servants and central DHSS administration there is misinformation and a patronising concern for people who are seen as hopeless victims. These attitudes, taken together, preclude any comprehensive or effective policy formulation. In the local offices, there appears to be a combination of exhausting overwork and frequent hostility to single homeless people. This can mean that they often do not receive what little the system offers them.

It may be helpful to explain briefly how the administrative machine in this area works. The section of the DHSS responsible for policy on these issues is called SB3. It is responsible, amongst other things, for:

• the management and policy development of 'resettlement units' (see p 78);
• policy and SB regulations concerning boarders; and
• the secretary of state's 'welfare responsibility' for this category of claimants under section 27 of the Supplementary Benefits Act 1976.

SB3 is a small backwater of the DHSS. Its head, at assistant-secretary level, tends either to be a younger civil servant given his or her first senior responsibility, before moving rapidly on to a more important post, or an older person achieving responsibility, and a higher salary, before retirement. Policy in SB3 does not show any consistent path of development. It has moved in contradictory ways—presumably because of the conflicting pressures of expenditure cuts, prejudice against an unpopular group, and the press and public criticism that have surfaced at intervals about the effects of policies in this area and the poor record of their implementation.

Boarders

People are treated as boarders, within the SB system, if they are living in a hotel, guest house, hostel or lodging house, or if the place they are living in provides meals that are prepared and eaten on the premises.[2] The most recent (1984) statistics estimate that there were 181,500 people in this category, about 30 per cent of them elderly—an increase of 129,500 since 1979.[3] This overall figure covers pensioners living in private nursing and residential homes; people, including those with special needs such as alcoholism and drug-abuse, living in hostels run by voluntary organisations (often in association with a housing association); and homeless people living in commercial bed and breakfast establishments and lodging houses.

The normal procedure of paying an SB allowance for personal expenses (such as food, clothes, fuel, etc), and quite separately paying housing benefit (HB) to cover rent, cannot be applied to those for whom these two elements are incorporated in the overall board and lodging charge. 'Boarders', therefore, receive SB to pay for their accommodation, a fixed amount for each meal not included in that charge and a smaller amount for personal expenses (clothes, laundry, toiletries, etc).

The 1980 Social Security Act

Social Assistance, the review of the SB system undertaken in 1977-8 (see Chapter 1) did not consider benefits for boarders. A second part to the review,[4] which would consider them, together with the question of resettlement units (then called reception centres, see p 78), was promised — but it never appeared. A consultation paper on boarders' benefits, published in late 1979,[5] just suggested that the current system continue, without considering any other options. Apparently, the DHSS had no ideas for a fairer system which would meet people's needs more adequately. CPAG's response[6] argued for a comprehensive change, incorporating boarders into the main SB system, with extra payments for additional requirements such as meal costs.

The November 1980 reforms of SB were broadly derived from *Social Assistance*, and so made no significant improvements to boarders' benefits. Regulations under the Act made explicit in law the previously discretionary restrictions of 'local board and lodging limits'.[7] This meant that the total amount for accommodation and meals (but not for personal expenses) was limited to a maximum set by each local DHSS office, taking account of charges for that type of accommodation in its area. The adjudication officer at local level thus retained considerable discretion, and the experience of advisers and voluntary organisations since 1980 suggests that this has been used in a steadily more restrictive way.

Unlike other rented accommodation, there is a relatively closed and unregulated market of lodgings and hotel or bed and breakfast accommodation which caters almost exclusively for DHSS claimants —as local social security staff are well aware. The charges are determined to some extent by the maximum the DHSS will pay. Thus, the local board and lodging limit has been used as an indirect and inappropriate means of controlling charges for this type of accommodation. If the limit is set below the level charged by the better establishments, claimants are obliged to stay in the poorer quality, claimant-only accommodation. They have little or no choice, since other accommodation is scarce or expensive — if available at all. An easy monopoly for unscrupulous landlords is, therefore, created outside the scope of legislation intended to control rents and standards in private rented housing. Virtually the only direct and effective method of control would be to regulate rents and charges, but this is something the government seems unwilling to contemplate. Thus, the DHSS picks up the bill for the failure of housing policy on two counts: the lack of adequate accommodation for all who need it, and the lack of political will to exert direct control over board and lodging charges.

Claimants, advisers and organisations such as CHAR (the Campaign for Single Homeless People) complained regularly from 1980 on about the inadequacy of the arrangements. The general tone of DHSS headquarters' responses to complaints about local ceilings on board and lodging allowances was that this was a matter for benefit officers, who were 'independent adjudicating authorities'.[8] Local offices argued that since claimants were getting the money, they must be finding somewhere to stay. However, evidence was accumulating from throughout the country that these local limits did not begin to match the cost of decent quality temporary accommodation.

On 2 September 1982 police in Oxford arrested large numbers of people living in several lodging houses and charged them with fraud.[9] ‘Operation Major’, as this well-organised and well-publicised police ‘swoop’ was called, put homeless claimants under the spotlight (see pp 123-4). Unfortunately, it was the problem which homeless people on benefit represented—rather than the problems they faced—that was brought into glaring focus in this way. Whilst claimants were prosecuted for giving false addresses, there was a distinct reluctance to take action against the landlords involved, who were exploiting the system of local limits to make exorbitant charges for accommodation of an appalling standard. The then chairman of the Social Security Advisory Committee (SSAC), the late Sir Arthur Armitage, asked DHSS officials to reconsider the administration of these limits, but no change was made.[10]

A survey in London, carried out by the Central London Social Security Advisers Forum and Camden Housing Aid Centre in May 1983,[11] discovered that very few hotel and bed and breakfast rooms were available anywhere in central London at a charge at or below the DHSS maximum (then £54 per week). In the area of the Westminster DHSS office, which had at least 2,000 ‘boarder’ claimants, there were no single rooms available at all below the limit. All these people were, therefore, being forced to share rooms in some of London’s worst and most dangerous hotels. The survey indicated that for the board and lodging limit in central London to represent the maximum payable for accommodation of ‘no more than a suitable standard’,[12] it needed to be about £100 per week. Soon afterwards, the limit in some offices was raised to £70 per week; and later in the year, after a further review, it went up to nearer £100.[13]

The contact that CHAR had with ministers, social services departments and MPs during 1982 and 1983 suggested that DHSS ministers urgently wanted to stop what they considered to be an abuse and to cut SB expenditure yet again; however, civil servants and the SSAC argued that a more thorough review of the confused arrangements for board and lodging limits was needed. (At the same time, the DHSS found that for another group—those requiring special care — a maximum limit could not, in fact, be enforced. These claimants, covered under the same set of regulations, are mainly elderly people who, it could be argued, must have their hostel or nursing home charge paid, whatever the costs, because there is no alternative for them.)

New local limits

In 1983 new draft regulations were introduced.[14] Their purpose, according to the SSAC,[15] was to amend the present regulations in such a way as:

(a) to provide for three tiers of local limits, to be determined for each local office area or groups of areas, for:

(i) ordinary board and lodging for fit persons;

(ii) residential care homes for special groups, such as the elderly, the mentally and physically handicapped and the mentally ill;

(iii) private nursing homes;

(b) to consolidate the present range of additions payable to those who may have higher charges because of special needs into one single addition at a higher rate than any currently payable;

(c) to increase the limit payable for children aged 11 and over up to the adult local limit and to pay a maximum of 1½ times the child's normal scale rate for those under 11.

The DHSS, in submitting the proposed regulations, stated that:

> The Department believes that these arrangements will strike the right balance between meeting the needs of the great majority of people who claim supplementary benefit while living in board and lodging accommodation or homes and preventing excessive demands on public funds.[16]

It was the first of these three changes—to set a three-tier system of local limits—which, not surprisingly, attracted the most attention. The potential conflict between the two aims outlined by the DHSS could have a significant effect on claimants' standard of living and accommodation, as the SSAC's fears demonstrated:

> Our anxiety over the way in which the proposals might in practice be operated is influenced by the degree of dissatisfaction expressed by representative organisations with the adequacy of local limits at the moment. We understand from DHSS that because of concern about their low level, a review of the limits was instituted in the autumn of 1982. Yet a substantial body of evidence made available to us shows that in many inner-city areas, where there is likely to be most need for board and lodging accommodation, the limits set are still inadequate and bear little relation to the charges payable in accommodation which fulfils the guidance criteria laid down for officials to follow. We are glad that DHSS recognises this problem, since it is quite plain that a system where the claimant relies entirely on the reasonableness of the limits set cannot function unless those limits are both realistic and regularly reviewed.[17]

The secretary of state replied:

> The government accept the need for such an improvement [if the arrangements for board and lodging limits are to operate without causing hardship]. In particular, arrangements will be set up as the Committee suggested for regular monitoring at regional and central level of the limits and the way they are set... the guidance will emphasise that the limit should be set at the highest reasonable level and that supplementary benefit officers should consult housing aid associations and other bodies regularly involved in housing the homeless in setting the limits.[18]

The secretary of state also agreed to delay implementation of the changes in order to give claimants and landlords a longer time to adjust. Accordingly, it was in November 1983 that the DHSS introduced its amendment setting three limits: the highest applied to nursing homes; the next, to residential homes; and the lowest to all other accommodation. The first two groups catered almost exclusively for pensioners, who are seen as the 'deserving' poor. (The fact that hostels for recovering alcoholics and drug-abusers were excluded from the second category reinforced this feeling. Although the secretary of state said this was because their original inclusion was an 'unintended consequence' of the drafting of earlier regulations, to those concerned it appeared a punitive move.) New administrative instructions went to all DHSS local offices, asking for strict monitoring at regional and national level to ensure that realistic limits were set.[19] There were some long-overdue, and consequently massive, increases in these limits — the maximum for nursing homes shot up beyond £200 per week in many areas.

The backlash

For single homeless people trying to find a decent place to stay in bed and breakfast, the new regulations were good news. They could now look for a good standard of room, and pay for it. Unfortunately, it was also good news for unscrupulous landlords, who could put their charges up with the knowledge that they still had an easy monopoly. Some local authorities also appeared to be taking advantage of the new limits as an indirect means of privatising residential care for elderly people. This was noted by the Commons Social Services Select Committee, which said in July 1984:

> In 31 areas, limits of over £200 or more a week apply in respect of private nursing home places — eg, Paisley (£207), Neasden (£240) and Leytonstone (£295) . . . It may be — we have no evidence to prove it — that health and local authorities are deliberately directing the elderly in need of residential care into the private sector where the non-cash-limited funds of supplementary benefit can foot the bill.[20]

Once again, the DHSS seemed to be absorbing the cost of cutbacks in other areas — on this occasion, the increased pressure on local authorities to restrict spending on their own provision of accommodation for the elderly. Tony Newton, then DHSS junior minister, commented rather lamely on this development: 'The apparent effect of the regulation change introduced last November was one which was not entirely expected by us.'[21]

Another consequence, presumably not entirely expected by the DHSS, was the strain put on voluntary organisations' hostels. In recognition of their high running costs, hostels built by a housing association and managed by a voluntary organisation can claim a hostel deficit grant from the DoE.[22] To control its costs, the DoE has always insisted that hostels charge a rent at least equal to the local DHSS limit, which the DoE assumed was the 'average' for local hostel accommodation. When the limits were increased in November 1983 to represent a maximum charge, without the fallback arrangement that had previously been available in special cases,[23] voluntary organisations' hostels were put in the position of being forced by the DoE to charge an amount that would put them in profit, in order to be able to claim a grant for their 'deficit'. Civil servants in SB3 later admitted that no one in the DHSS had thought to tell the DoE of the policy change.[24] Meanwhile, hostel budgets were in total disarray. Worse still, just as this mess was being cleared up, the DHSS proposed amendments which would have turned either voluntary hostels or their residents into paupers, as explained below.

The *Daily Express* of 4 November 1983 thought that the increase in limits was sensational news. Its headline screamed: 'Scandal of £100 dole drop-outs'. The story went on to quote anonymous 'charity workers' saying that 'young drifters are lured to London by high benefits, which many spend on drink, drugs and gambling'. The Press Council took six months to dismiss a complaint from Conservative MP Charles Irving, chairperson of the All-Party Committee for the Homeless and Rootless, that the report was ill-informed nonsense. The Press Council was apparently satisfied that such a charity worker did exist and did make those comments.[25]

Government ministers, to their credit, appeared to defend the decision to increase limits[26]—that is, until Dr Rhodes Boyson, then DHSS minister, said that he believed that high levels of benefit for temporary accommodation could encourage young people to leave home, and that this damaged family life. The issue of benefits and young people is dealt with in detail in Chapter 7. Here, just let it be said that it is alarming that a man with such decided views chaired the review into benefits for children and young people (until moved to the Northern Ireland Office).

Just as the furore over the limits was dying down, another 'problem' was discovered — that of people being paid 'so much' in some temporary accommodation that they were 'unwilling' to move into a permanent home of their own.[27] Again, it was voluntary organisations' hostels which were the target of intended restrictions — the same hostels which the DoE had been encouraging as part of its three-year 'hostels initiative', and which SB3 was promoting to replace the old Camberwell resettlement unit (see p 78).

In a new set of draft regulations, submitted to the SSAC in March 1984,[28] it was therefore proposed that claimants who were living in hostels, hotels, lodging houses or similar establishments should be excluded from the definition of a boarder, if there were adequate facilities to enable residents to prepare their own meals and if the board charge did not include the provision of any meals. A quick calculation by CHAR on the day the proposals were announced showed that this would leave a claimant living in a hostel where breakfast and dinner were provided with £1.70 per week to buy lunches, clothes and all other requirements. SB3, when challenged about this, admitted that it had not thought of this consequence.[29]

The SSAC received its biggest-ever response to consultation on these proposed amendments — and it was overwhelmingly and vehemently critical. In its report, the SSAC commented:

> We have been much struck by the range of organisations who have written to us about the effects of the proposal on accommodation ranging from sheltered housing projects for the elderly to rehabilitation hostels for the mentally ill and mentally handicapped as well as every type of housing for the single homeless.[30]

And it concluded:

> Whatever the merits of the proposed amendment in principle, it is plain that it would cause quite disproportionate problems for hostels, their residents and for local authorities, and would moreover have a substantial impact on community care and voluntary projects of the kind the government have been seeking to encourage. We could therefore not accept that the proposal should be proceeded with in its present form.[31]

The DHSS withdrew the proposal, but with the face-saving threat that the government

> believes that there are a number of possible modifications which might do much to meet the concerns that have been expressed. But it will be important, as the Committee pointed out, to examine carefully the possible impact of any revised proposal

> on all the various interests involved, and this will inevitably take a little time.[32]

Both the DHSS and SSAC have suggested that this was a matter that the current social security reviews would be considering.[33]

As part of the latest instalment in these policy changes, the DHSS announced on 5 September 1984[34] that it was to freeze all board and lodging limits at their 1984 level until the spring of 1985, at the earliest, and that ministers would bring to parliament an amendment giving them, instead of local 'independent adjudicating authorities', the power to fix all local limits. Whilst these interim emergency powers were in force, the DHSS would introduce 'proposals for more lasting arrangements for setting the maximum . . . which will be put into operation when the interim measures lapse'. On 12 November 1984 draft regulations were announced, transferring the discretionary power, and Norman Fowler elaborated on cuts to be made to benefits paid to boarders following the Chancellor's Autumn Statement.

Two and a half weeks later, the DHSS issued a consultation paper on the proposed changes. If implemented in April 1985, as the government intends, the proposed restrictions will seriously disrupt the lives of tens of thousands of homeless claimants. For ordinary board and lodging, the government intends to restrict those who are eligible to be boarders and reduce the total amounts they can receive. In London, the weekly limit will be reduced to £70 (from £100 in some areas), which allows only £48.30 for bed and breakfast. Elsewhere, the limit will be £50-£60 (as low as £28.30 for bed and breakfast). The limit for a couple will only be 1½ or 1¾ times that for a single person.

In restricting eligibility, the consultation paper reinforces the 'parish test' of the Elizabethan and Victorian Poor Laws:

> For unemployed people without dependants claiming benefit *outside their normal local office area*, the government is proposing new rules limiting the period for which benefit is paid... Ministers regard it as reasonable to make payment on a board and lodging basis for between two and four weeks in a particular locality. Thereafter payment would be reduced to the non-householder rate (£22.45) unless a claimant can show that householder status (£28.05) is justified (emphasis added).[35]

Exceptions are to be allowed for 'long-standing' unemployed boarders — presumably older hostel dwellers. Young people (under 18), on the other hand, will only be allowed benefit as boarders in exceptional circumstances (ie, if they are pregnant or with children; if they have been in care and there is no family home to go to; if they are handicapped; if they were previously living in board and lodging while employed; and, if none of these applies, where it may be the 'only means of preventing serious risk or serious damage to [their] health and safety'). Otherwise, they will be restricted to the non-householder rate of £17.30 per week for all their needs (housing, food, fuel, clothes, laundry, etc). New restrictions will also apply to payments made to those living in residential care homes and nursing homes.

There is no doubt that these measures are punitive, simply intended to stop claimants living in board and lodging. The government wrongly assumes that claimants have a choice. Housing campaign groups have explained the increase in boarder claimants from 52,000 in 1979 to 181,500 in 1984 as a consequence of cuts in housing expenditure since 1979.[36] The standard of board and lodging accommodation is not so tempting as to attract masses of additional claimants to flock to it from their homes. Rather, it is the combination of the government's failure to tackle unemployment and to increase the stock of adequate, cheap housing for those on low incomes which has caused the recent upsurge in the numbers of board and lodging claimants — who are then penalised for making 'excessive demands on public [DHSS] funds' (see p 71). It should also be noted that there has not been a substantial rise in board and lodging charges; indeed, the percentage increase in 1984 is the lowest for five years.[37]

Single homeless people

Board and lodging limits, as pointed out above, apply both to homeless claimants living as boarders and to the elderly in need of residential care. Thus, two groups, one 'undeserving' and the other 'deserving' in popular imagery, are covered by the same regulations. This fact may go some way to explaining the twists and turns of government policy in trying to find a solution to the 'problem' of overspending without causing offence to the 'deserving' group.

The end of the welfare state line, however, is reached by those who have nowhere to live at all — not even an establishment from which to claim board and lodging payments. Less concern is shown when dealing with these people — to groups working in the field, DHSS policy seems to be characterised by a penny-pinching concern for costs and an indifference to the circumstances of homeless people. This section looks briefly at three aspects of this: the benefit rates themselves; the special DHSS offices for homeless people; and the resettlement units.

Benefit rates

Single homeless claimants found themselves the target of a sudden cut in their benefit rates in 1980. Until then, homeless people sleeping rough were paid benefit equal to the sum of the boarders' meals allowances. The November 1980 SB reforms cut their benefit to the non-householder's rate.[38] Patrick Jenkin, then Secretary of State for Social Services, explained:

> It seems anomalous that persons without any accommodation at all are paid more benefit than non-householders contributing to their upkeep in a relative's home. Whilst it is commonly dearer to eat in commercial establishments than in private ones, there are other aspects of household expenses, such as fuel and rent, to which the non-householder's benefit is also applied...
>
> It was felt that a non-householder would have cause to feel aggrieved if he saw that a person could get more actual cash in hand by being homeless (sometimes by choice) than by contributing towards the cost of a household and accepting the attendant responsibilities.[39]

Jenkin failed completely to appreciate the high cost of eating out all the time. The comparison with non-householders is disingenuous. They received an extra £2.15 per week in 1980 (£3.30 in 1984/85) precisely in order to pay for their contribution to the household costs. The pitiful amount of money that homeless single people were expected to live on caused even the *Daily Telegraph* to describe their £18.90 per week (in 1982) as 'grindingly little'.[40] The cut in benefit was restored in July 1983,[41] after repeated pressure from concerned groups. So the amount of benefit that single homeless people now receive at least covers the cost of food. But there is still no recognition of the additional costs of other aspects of personal expenditure (eg, clothing, toiletries, etc).

Local offices

Other chapters of this book describe the collapse of the DHSS's local office service, in particular the strikes provoked by understaffing and overwork. For people with nowhere to stay, as well as no money, that collapse in administration is all the more harmful. When payments and interviews are delayed and people cannot book into temporary accommodation, health and even lives are put at risk.

There are two special offices in London, and another in Glasgow, set up to deal with single homeless male claimants alone. The special offices are intended by the DHSS to serve three purposes: to provide greater control of claims, which frequently alter (and therefore have fraud potential); to provide a better service for the complex needs of single homeless claimants; and to protect other claimants who have been upset 'by the appearance and habits of men living in hostels and lodging houses'.[42]

The record of both these special offices, and of local offices generally, in delivering benefits to this category of claimant is poor. For example, a take-up campaign between May and September 1983 amongst Glasgow's 2,000 lodging-house residents uncovered approximately £1m in arrears of SB. Residents were each being underpaid between £7.50 and about £17.00 per week because no additional requirements were being paid.[43] And in London, a take-up campaign limited to laundry additions (payable because people are unable to do their washing safely in institutions for the homeless) had an 80 per cent success rate amongst several thousand claimants. In one lodging-house, two men each discovered that they were owed over £1,000 by the DHSS.[44]

Resettlement units
These are the government-run institutions, descendants of the old 'casual wards' under the Poor Law, which provide extremely basic accommodation for 'people without a settled way of life'. Called 'reception centres' until 1980, they were commonly known among their residents as 'spikes'. From Beveridge's day until the early 1970s, DHSS policy was to close as many of these as possible. The expectation was that accommodation would be provided instead by social services department or voluntary organisation hostels, on a smaller, less institutional scale. Despite some difficulties, this policy was successful overall. Only 23 resettlement units remain of the 270 casual wards/reception centres that existed in England and Wales in 1948.[45] However, almost nothing happened in resettlement unit policy for over a decade during the 1970s, except the decision to close the most notorious, Camberwell, in 1985, when the lease on this former workhouse runs out. Other units, in Nissen huts and other makeshift sites, continue to deteriorate, becoming ever more irrelevant to the policies being developed to address the needs of homeless single people.

Policy papers and decisions on the future of all the resettlement units have been promised regularly since 1979. In 1982-83 Tony Newton promised at quarterly intervals that a consultative document would be published.[46] It is still to appear—though as this book went to print, he again promised that such a document would be issued, early in 1985.[47] One explanation for this silence which appears to fit the facts well is that the DHSS fears the Treasury will want to 'save' any money that ceases to be spent on resettlement units directly and will not allow it to be transferred to other similar budgets. This is yet another example of the rigidity—indeed paralysis — in policy-making induced by the cost-cutting ethos of this government.

Conclusion

The history of the treatment of boarders and the homeless graphically demonstrates the muddled administration and the poor quality of policy-making now endemic in the DHSS. Ministers have responded to press campaigns and pressures from backbenchers to produce 'magic solutions' by initiating changes which make matters worse rather than better. Creative thinking on how to solve the problems has been paralysed by the knowledge not only that no extra money will be made available, but also that money 'saved' is likely to be siphoned away from the DHSS budget altogether.

This chapter has demonstrated, however, that not all the blame can be laid at the door of the DHSS itself—despite its tendency to fall in with prejudiced attitudes against groups such as the single homeless, seen as 'undeserving' claimants. The crises may manifest themselves in the panic measures so often taken recently by DHSS ministers and officials in this area of policy and administration. Yet the roots of the problems often lie elsewhere: in the government's failure to reduce unemployment; in the drastic cuts in housing expenditure in recent years; and in the refusal to take direct measures to control board and lodging charges. The bill for these failures is being paid for by one of the most vulnerable sectors of society. Even as an exercise in crisis management, this is completely inadequate; as an attempt at humanity, it is a cruel deception.

References

1 *Single and Homeless*, Department of Environment, HMSO 1981, Table 16.
2 Reg 9(13), Supplementary Benefit (Requirements) Regulations 1983.
3 Taken from DHSS press release, 5 September 1984, and DHSS consultation paper, *Supplementary Benefit for Board and Lodging Payments*, 1984.
4 *Social Assistance: a review of the supplementary benefit scheme in Great Britain*, DHSS 1978, Annex I, AI.8.
5 DHSS consultation paper, *Review of the Supplementary Benefits Scheme: boarders and people in residential accommodation*, 1979.
6 *Claimants on the Edge of the System*, CPAG 1980.
7 Regs 9(6) and 9(7), Supplementary Benefit (Requirements) Regulations 1983.
8 Letter from the Chief Supplementary Benefit Officer to the Central London Social Security Advisers Forum, 12 May 1982.
9 For a full account of Operation Major, read Ros Franey, *Poor Law*, CHAR, CPAG, Oxford Claimants Union et al 1983, and *Operation Major: an assessment*, CHAR 1983.
10 Letter to CHAR, 25 October 1982.
11 'The sort I'm trying to get rid of', Central London Social Security Advisers Forum 1983.
12 Reg 9(6), Supplementary Benefits (Requirements) Regulations 1983.
13 Central London Social Security Advisers Forum *Newssheet*, July 1983.

14 Supplementary Benefit (Requirements) Amendment Regulations 1983.
15 *Reports of the Social Security Advisory Committee in accordance with Section 10(3) of the Social Security Act 1980 preceded by a Statement made by the Secretary of State for Social Services in accordance with Section 10(4) of that Act*, Cmnd 8978, July 1983.
16 See note 15, p 29, para 14.
17 See note 15, p 27, para 6.
18 See note 15, p 4, para 4.
19 Reproduced in Cmnd 8978 (see note 15 above), pp 30-31.
20 House of Commons, *Select Committee on Social Services Fourth Report for the Session 1983-4 on Public Expenditure in the Social Services* (July 1984), paras 60 and 61, p xxvii.
21 See note 20 above, reply to question no G 80.
22 These grants are given under section 33 of the Housing Act 1974.
23 Under Reg 9(5), Supplementary Benefit (Requirements) Regulations 1983.
24 Meeting between CHAR and officials of the DHSS and DoE, 22 May 1984.
25 Report of the Press Council, 1984.
26 Letter to David Knox MP, 17 January 1984.
27 'Changes in Supplementary Benefit Regulations', press release from the SSAC, 2 April 1984.
28 Supplementary Benefit (Requirements and Resources) Amendment Regulations 1984.
29 In a telephone conversation between a member of CHAR staff and an SB3 official.
30 *Reports of the Social Security Advisory Committee in accordance with Section 10(3) of the Social Security Act 1980 preceded by a Statement made by the Secretary of State for Social Services in accordance with Section 10(4) of that Act*, Cmnd 9296, 1984, p 20, para 12.
31 See note 30 above, p 21, para 13.
32 See note 30 above, Statement by the Secretary of State, p 6, para 11.
33 See note 30 above, p 6, para 12.
34 DHSS press release, 5 September 1984.
35 DHSS consultative document, *Supplementary Benefit Board and Lodging Payments*, 30 November 1984.
36 *The Times*, 1 December 1984.
37 See note 35 above, Annex.
38 Reg 6 and Schedule 2, para 4, Supplementary Benefit (Requirements) Regulations 1980.
39 Letters from Patrick Jenkin to Rt Hon Reg Freeson MP, 7 October 1980 and 3 June 1981.
40 *Daily Telegraph*, Leader, 7 September 1982.
41 Under the Supplementary Benefit Amendment Regulations 1983, which amended the 1980 (Requirements) Regulations, SI No 1299, Schedule 2, para 4.
42 *House of Commons Hansard*, 25 May 1979, col 322W.
43 A full account of this campaign, run by Strathclyde Welfare Rights Officers, can be found in *Maladministration of Benefits: the Glasgow hostel campaign*, CHAR 1984.
44 DHSS London North letters to CHAR 14 February, 20 March, 4 May, 11 June 1984.
45 *House of Commons Hansard*, 21 July 1983, col 211W.
46 Letter to CHAR 11 November 1982, letter to Brynmor John MP 3 June 1983, and *House of Commons Hansard*, 21 July 1983, col 211W.
47 Personal communication.

7. Seen but not heard: **young people**

JANET ALLBESON

In November 1980 the government implemented rules abolishing supplementary benefit (SB) for school-leavers in the weeks immediately after they left school.[1] The proposal to abolish SB for school-leavers had first been made in *Social Assistance*, under a Labour administration (see Chapter 1). But, in a number of ways, this benefit cut was perhaps more important as an indication of Conservative cuts to come.

Justifying the loss of benefit to school-leavers, the then minister for social security argued:

> . . . however important is each group in our society that receives benefit from time to time, for whatever reason, there are groups, hard-pressed families, to whom I would want to accord a higher priority than to school-leavers...if we have limited resources, we have to decide where those limited resources are to go and what benefits can be given to those who are hardest pressed.[2]

It was an ominous sign of Conservative thinking; if money needed to be found in the benefits system, young people ranked low on the list of groups to be protected. The loss of benefit to school-leavers saved over £3m.[3] In effect, it was achieved by official prolongation of the state of childhood. Newly unemployed school-leavers lost the right to claim SB independently until the start of the new term after they had left school, whilst their parents were allowed to keep dependent children's benefits—child benefit and dependency additions paid with other benefits—for the same period. It is interesting to note the distinction made by the minister between 'less deserving' school-leavers and more deserving 'hard-pressed families'. In fact, the savings to the state of withdrawing benefit were being met by parents, required to support their teenage children for up to three months longer.

Since 1980 the following trends have become increasingly apparent: the low priority attached to protecting the incomes of young people; the delay in recognition of adult independence for the unemployed by the state; and the transfer of support for those on benefit from the state to the family, with little acknowledgment of the financial burden that results. This chapter traces how the incomes of young people—both in and out of work—have been under attack in the last few years, and examines why young people and their families have little reason to be optimistic about the outcome of the social security review currently examining their circumstances. The chapter is divided into three parts: a summary of the cuts; an examination of why young people are an easy political target; and a description of the consequences of the government's measures.

The cuts so far

The young unemployed

As explained above, in November 1980 young people lost the right to claim SB immediately they left school. Instead, almost all young people were treated as dependants of their parents, who therefore received child benefit for them, until the start of the following term.[4] Distinctions were later made between school-leavers who were unemployed, and so treated as dependants, and those who were either employed or on a Youth Training Scheme (YTS), and so lost their 'dependent' status — from May 1982, child benefit ceased if a school-leaver obtained a job or a Manpower Services Commission (MSC) placement,[5] and from November 1984, a school-leaver's earnings or MSC training allowance have counted against any SB the parent receives for him/her.[6]

The introduction of housing benefit (HB) provided the excuse for further cuts. From April 1983 all 16- and 17-year-olds newly claiming SB were paid £3.10 per week *less* than 16- and 17-year-olds already receiving SB,[7] so that, instead of £18.90 per week, their benefit was reduced to only £15.80. The government justified this cut on the grounds that the £3.10 had been paid as a 'rent contribution' to 16- and 17-year-olds on top of the amount paid for ordinary living expenses. Under the new HB scheme, parents with 16- and 17-year-olds living at home would no longer have to demand £3.10 per week from their children, because their own HB would no longer be reduced by £3.10 in respect of the teenagers.[8] Thus, argued the government, lower income families (ie, those dependent on HB) were no worse off: the £3.10 removed from 16- and 17-year-olds reappeared, in effect, as an extra amount of HB paid to the parent. The same argument was used a year later, in April 1984,[9] when the SB of 18- to 20-year-olds was cut by £3.10,[10] while their parents' HB was increased (or would have been but for other cuts made simultaneously) by the same amount. This time, however, there were no transitional provisions to cushion existing beneficiaries—all 18- to 20-year-olds on benefit saw their money drop from £24.55 to £21.45 per week. For young people aged 16 to 20 living in families where HB was not in payment, the loss of the £3.10 rent contribution was a real drop, not only in their income but in the contribution they could give their parents. Altogether, there was a net saving to the government from the abolition of rent additions for 16- to 20-year-olds of £73m in a full year.[11]

Youth Training Scheme

In December 1981 the government published a White Paper[12] announcing the Youth Training Scheme (YTS). Designed to replace the Youth Opportunities Programme, it came into operation in September 1983. However, the terms under which the government wanted YTS to operate were controversial. It was proposed that the new scheme be made compulsory, by removing the right to claim SB from everyone who left school at the minimum age until the first Monday in the September of the following year. The training allowance of £14.40 a week paid to participants would be below the SB level for 16-year-olds (£15.80 at that time).

Widespread opposition to these proposals meant that they were taken no further. However, in a bid to provide a disincentive to 16-year-olds thinking of refusing or giving up a YTS place, the government introduced the 'work-shy' penalty of a 40 per cent reduction in benefit for six weeks for 16-year-olds who opted out of a YTS placement. It was possible to do this under existing legislation. All the Secretary of State for Employment was required to do was to announce that he had approved YTS as training 'for the purpose of becoming or keeping fit for entry into, or return to, regular employment'.[13] Thus, the old 'work-shy' penalty, used against the unemployed since 1911,[14] could automatically be extended to 16-year-olds refusing or giving up a training scheme placement.

Although the attempt to pitch a training allowance for 16-year-olds at below SB level failed, the government has reduced the value of the allowance simply by refusing to up-rate it. The following figures show the increases in the YOP/YTS weekly allowance since 1978: April 1978 £19.50, November 1978 £20.55, November 1979 £23.50, January 1982 £25.00, and November 1984 £26.25. Had the allowance kept its real value, it would now be worth £35.76 per week; had it been increased at the same rate as earnings, it would be worth £39.71.[15]

Young workers

It would appear that the government has had a consistent policy of trying to lower the earnings of young people, who, it considers, have priced themselves out of jobs. For instance, in January 1982 it introduced the Young Workers Scheme. Under this, employers get a subsidy of up to £15 per week for each person they employ under 18 who is paid less than £50 a week. In October 1983 107,000 young people were on the scheme. Although this is not a large number, it seems to have had the effect of depressing young people's wages overall. In the first full year of the scheme (April 1982 to April 1983), earnings for under 18-year-olds rose by 1.8 per cent for males and 3.2 per cent for females, compared with adult wage rises of 8.4 per cent and 9.2 per cent respectively.[16]

Although young people under 21 on SB are now no longer expected to make a contribution to the rent whilst living at home, young working people living at home whose parents are on HB have seen the contribution they are expected to pay towards the rent rise dramatically. Their rent contribution is enforced by deductions from the parents' HB—called 'non-dependant deductions'. The figures below show the rises in non-dependant deductions (per week) for working young people since April 1983.

Working non-dependant	*April 1983*	*April 1984*	*November 1984*
aged 16-17	nil	nil	£3.30
aged 18-20	£5.55	£8.20	£8.80
aged 21+	£6.55	£8.20	£8.80

Studying while unemployed

The present government has made persistent attempts to draw a dividing line between the genuine student, who is not entitled to SB, and the unemployed person studying as a fill-in measure whilst looking for work, who may be able to get SB. The absence of jobs for young people has meant that the distinction between the two categories has become increasingly difficult to maintain. Unable to test a student claimant's willingness to work by the offer of a job, the Department of Health and Social Security (DHSS) has instead resorted to elaborate rules to exclude from benefit all those it considers not genuinely unemployed. From November 1980 unemployed people could continue to receive SB whilst studying, provided (a) they remained able and willing to take a job, (b) the course was a non-advanced one of fewer than 21 hours a week, and (c) they had not left a job, or school, to join the course. Claimants aged 21 or more also had to have been unemployed and receiving SB for 12 months before the course began.[17]

The '21-hour rule', as it came to be known, allowed many young people to undertake courses, such as O and A levels, which were very similar, if not identical, to the courses they would have done had they not left school and become unemployed. Thus, two young people of the same age could study side by side for A levels, one of them qualifying for benefit and the other not.

Alarmed at the large numbers of young people who could potentially claim benefit, with very little chance of their willingness to work ever being put to the test, in March 1982 the DHSS sought to impose new restrictions. Rather than change the law, however, it resorted to a secret internal circular,[18] advising benefit officers to count meal breaks and the hours spent doing homework as part of a course. The result was that benefit was withdrawn from young people on courses where the hours of teaching alone never approached the 21-hour mark. Some courses, set up specially for the unemployed under the 21-hour rule, suddenly collapsed. Not surprisingly, the DHSS's interpretation of the '21-hour rule' was challenged and was finally rejected by a tribunal of Social Security Commissioners, who declared the DHSS's approach to be incorrect in July 1982.[19]

The government then moved to change the law itself. In August 1982 it introduced amendments to the 21-hour rule which accepted that the calculation of the length of a course should ignore meal breaks and private study, but introduced a qualifying period of three months' unemployment for people wishing to study under the 21-hour rule.[20] This represented an improvement for people aged 19 or over, but its real purpose was surely to alleviate the fears of the DHSS that too many young people were getting benefit who were not unemployed.

There was widespread criticism of this new condition. It was pointed out that someone who left school in June did not become officially unemployed until the following September.[21] As a result of the three-month rule, s/he would not qualify to study part-time until December—five or six months after leaving school. In response to these criticisms, the government argued that school-leavers could still study part-time if the DHSS (in particular, the child benefit section) accepted they were not in 'full-time education'. The child benefit authorities had decided that full-time education meant a course of more than 15 hours including homework and meal breaks.[22]

This '15-hour rule'—an administrative invention, with no basis in law—was also challenged and rejected. A Social Security Commissioner, in a decision first publicised in March 1984, decided that a claimant doing a course of 13½ hours' teaching plus five hours' private study was not studying full-time.[23] However, despite the fact that Commissioners' decisions are binding on all future decisions on the same matter, in a further circular the DHSS in April 1984 advised its staff to ignore this decision.[24] But the government again resorted to legislation to win the battle conclusively. From August 1984 a person under 19 who has not been unemployed for three months (and therefore is not eligible for benefit under the 21-hour rule) can study for a maximum of *12 hours* a week, excluding time spent in private study and meal breaks.[25]

An easy target

It is never easy to separate the ideological justifications for cuts made in public by the politicians from the coldly pragmatic considerations which, behind the scenes, make certain areas of public expenditure more vulnerable to 'savings' than others. Where young people are concerned, the two are very much intertwined.

In the summer of 1983 extensive leaks revealed that Treasury ministers were pushing for cuts in young people's benefits. According to *The Economist:*

> Some ministers appear to favour larger cuts in the dole more narrowly directed at unemployed young people. At first sight there is a stronger case for this on public spending grounds. There are 721,000 people on the dole and living with their parents. Those aged 16-17 years receive £15.80 a week, and those who are 18 or over get £23.65. If these rates were cut back to the £13.15 for each child (aged 11-15) paid to unemployed parents, the savings could add up to around £300m a year.[26]

As the *Guardian* pointed out: 'These savings do not look negligible especially when put beside the £13 million a year which could be cut from unemployment benefit—or £40 million from supplementary benefit and unemployment benefit—for each 1 per cent point real cut.'[27] According to *The Times*, the motive behind such cuts would be:

> primarily to allow the DHSS to offer a meaty sacrifice on the altar of the Public Expenditure Survey Committee. This, from Whitehall's point of view, has the merit of being seen to hurt (the Treasury is never convinced unless there are screams) but also, more important for the long run, to establish the violability of basic social benefits and do it for a group over which the political screams will not be too loud.[28]

The Treasury arguments for cuts in young people's benefits on public expenditure grounds certainly coincide neatly with calls for an increased role for the family. The ideology behind the reduction in young people's incomes — both in and out of work — has two strands: Conservative views on the role of the family and a belief, in the face of all the evidence, that lower incomes will create more jobs.

The Conservatives believe that the family should take care of its own. As Sir Keith Joseph put it: 'Inasmuch as personal responsibility has been eroded by a shift of housing, education and welfare provision excessively to the state, we are trying to shift that balance.'[29] Leaks to the *Guardian* from the Cabinet's Family Policy Group in February 1983 revealed that one of its aims was to look at 'what more could be done to encourage families—in the widest sense—to reassume...responsibility for the disabled, elderly [and] unemployed 16-year-olds'.[30]

Behind the cuts in young people's benefits since 1980, and the rapid rise in rent contributions expected from working teenagers living at home whose parents are on HB, can be seen the re-establishment of the idea of the family as a single interdependent unit. As in other areas of welfare provision, such as social services, families — both parents and children — are being asked to pay the price of cuts in state support.

Low benefit levels have always meant that unemployed teenagers have been subsidised to some extent by their parents. However, the loss of the £3.10 per week rent contribution for 16- to 20-year-olds represents the official sanctioning of their dependence. In effect, parents with unemployed children have been told by the government that they must provide free accommodation for their offspring. 'A young person without a job, on supplementary benefit,' said the Secretary of State for Social Services, 'will often be living in a household with parents who will not need to look to him for a contribution towards housing costs.'[31]

In the case of parents on HB, the transference of £3.10 (now £3.30) a week from unemployed child to parent meant no change to the finances of the household as a whole. But it did mean a change in responsibility: the young person was no longer in charge of paying (or not paying) a contribution towards the rent. Instead, the parent was forced by the government into the position of provider.

The large rent contributions that working teenagers are now expected to pay can mean that if there is more than one working child, the whole of their parent's rent can be taken up by their assumed contribution, when the parent is on HB. The view of the family as a single entity is perhaps best seen in the fact that the *child's* expected contribution to the rent is enforced by deducting the equivalent amount from the *parent's* benefit. The government can argue that there is nothing new in 'non-dependant deductions' from rent and rate rebates, but never before have these deductions reached such a significant level that they distort the normal balance of financial responsibility between parent and child. In addition, the enforcement of working teenagers' responsibilities to their parents is confined to the less well-off, that is, to families on HB. The government has made no moves to encourage working teenagers to contribute towards their parents' mortgage by making non-dependant deductions from mortgage interest tax relief.

Preventing the break-up of the family is one of the major reasons given for government ministers' current anxieties about young unemployed people who, on leaving home, can instantly be given full benefit towards their housing costs, and considerably more for living expenses than if they remained with their parents. A number of 'scare stories' have appeared in the press, pointing out the huge rise in income obtained by youngsters who leave home and move into bed and breakfast accommodation. In May 1984, for instance, the *Daily Telegraph* reported that a spate of burglaries and shop-lifting in Newquay, Cornwall, was being blamed on an influx of unemployed young people from Liverpool. The Chief Inspector of Newquay police was reported as saying: 'They like it down here because they can pick up £51.60 a week . . . but not all of the people who come down here are of good character.'[32]

The Times reported that the Grand Hotel in Dawlish was advertising for unemployed residents:

> [The hotelier] tells guests to register the Grand, which has 24 bedrooms, as their home and the Department of Health and Social Security will pay the rent. 'They get a total of about £70 a week, so it leaves them with quite a lot of pocket money.'... Mr Martin B. . . aged 21 from Stockport said: 'It is absolutely great. Far better than trudging the dirty streets at home looking for work.'[33]

Finally, there was the case of two mothers in Peterborough who swapped sons, apparently arousing the ire of ministers concerned. Instead of living with their mothers as 'non-householders', the two boys, by changing their addresses, were able to claim benefit as commercial boarders, thus receiving £51 a week instead of £21.45.[34]

Leaks at the time of the 1983 annual public spending round identified the payment of rent allowances to young claimants as a major target for cuts. The *Sunday Times* reported that ministers believed such payments encouraged the break-up of families and the abuse of social security benefits. 'They have been shocked by tales of jobless youngsters removing to cheap winter lettings at holiday resorts to enjoy a life of doubtful morality at the state's expense.'[35]

In November 1984 the government acted, by proposing changes from April 1985 to limit both the categories of SB claimants eligible for board and lodging payments and the amounts they can receive. (Fuller details of the proposals are given in Chapter 6.) The most draconian changes, however, are reserved for 16- and 17-year-olds. If the government's suggestions are accepted, these teenagers will no longer be able to claim benefit to cover the costs of living away from home—unless they come within a shortlist of special categories (see pp 75-6). Almost all 16- and 17-year-olds, therefore, will be forced to continue living at home with their parent(s), regardless of their family circumstances. Unemployed young people of 18 and older will only be able to claim board and lodging payments for two to four weeks before facing stringent tests of eligibility.

As a *Times* editorial on 15 December pointed out, these measures, in seeking 'to discourage young jobless from moving', are 'suited to a sclerotic nation ... [measures] to freeze jobs and people'. *The Times* likened the proposals to the old Poor Law, which prevented the poor from moving outside their own parish, and quoted approvingly from Adam Smith's criticisms of such restrictions on the free movement of labour. Unemployed young people who obey Norman Tebbit's injunction to get on their bikes to look for work will in future be told to pedal home again—even if 'home' is an unhappy family situation in an area of high unemployment.

The fact that young people can simply remove themselves from parental support by leaving home has also been given as a reason for the current restrictions on access to furniture grants for single people. The majority of single people needing furniture grants are *not* teenagers who have just left home, but the government insists that, if it changed its current restrictive policy, 'the family unit would not be encouraged. It would instead encourage people to move away from the family after the slightest argument and it would be costly.'[36] On this issue, at least, the appeal to Conservative values on the family is shown to be inseparable from public spending considerations.

The second strand of Conservative philosophy underpinning the government's attitude to young people is a belief that lower incomes among the young would lead to more jobs and fewer unemployed people. High wage and benefit levels are seen as partly responsible for the present massive extent of youth unemployment. 'Because the wages of young people are often too high in relation to experienced adults,' said the Prime Minister in 1981, 'employers cannot afford to take them on—even though it is clear that many employers want to help.'[37] A Department of Employment research paper, published in early 1984, purported to show that young people's employment prospects could be improved if their wages were cut.[38] It concluded that up to 100,000 jobs could be created for young people by a 10 per cent cut in their wages.

Closer scrutiny of the report revealed that this would be largely at the expense of jobs for adult workers. Nevertheless, the government continues to suggest that moves to depress youth wages are very much on the agenda. Chancellor of the Exchequer Nigel Lawson was reported in September 1984 to be 'planning a package of job creation measures aimed at keeping wage rates down to provide more low-paid jobs particularly for the young'.[39] In the wake of the September 1984 unemployment figures, showing 103,900 school-leavers yet to find work, the government has also set up a working party under David Young—the Cabinet minister with special responsibility for job creation measures—to report on the training, education and employment of 14- to 18-year-olds (see p 94).

If the 'low wage' policy for young people is to be effective, then benefit levels for young people are obviously relevant. In an interview given soon after her last election victory, the Prime Minister was asked whether she agreed that unemployment among school-leavers would be reduced only by decreasing the wages of the young. Revealingly, Margaret Thatcher's answer dealt with *benefit* levels:

> It really has been my dream to have unemployment not an option for the young, so that they either stay at school or go into further education, or into a job or into some form of training. It has been my dream that unemployment should not be an option...
>
> It's too easy for some of them, straight out of school, to go straight on to social security at the age of 16. They like it, they have a lot of money and some of them, not all of them by a long chalk, but some of them, learn a way of life they should never have a chance to learn.[40]

A month later, the Chancellor said: 'There can be no doubt whatever that at the margin there are people, even in present circumstances, who take a rational decision that it is not worth their while taking a job at the sort of pay at which jobs would be on offer.'[41]

The depression of youth wages would have to be very severe indeed to bring them near to the £16.50 per week currently paid to 16- to 17-year-olds, or the £21.45 paid to 18- to 20-year-olds, living with their parents. Nevertheless, the 'incentive effect' of lower benefit levels for young people is evidently being taken very seriously by the government — even though there is considerable evidence that higher wage levels for young people would do far more to achieve the government's aims (see pp 95-6).

The government may well have been helped in its determination by the lack of any organised resistance to the cuts there have been so far. As *The Times* has pointed out:

> The elderly not only have votes and lobbyists but a range of formidable allies including several of the most venerable attractions of the upper House of Parliament. Children have no votes;

> they rely shakily on politicians' sense of family. When children become adolescents, their political interest declines even further, until they become old enough to vote.[42]

There appears to be little to fear from the young themselves, even those old enough to vote. At the last election, a National Opinion Poll of more than 1,000 first-time voters showed that although 79 per cent identified unemployment as the most significant issue, a majority said they intended to vote Conservative.[43] A research project on young unemployed people in the North-east found that political action around the issue of unemployment was conspicuous by its absence. One of the ways young people cope with being unemployed is by trying to forget it.[44] The research suggests that the majority of young people react to unemployment by becoming apathetic and depressed, rather than by involving themselves in activities aimed at challenging the situation.

The real world: the effect of the cuts

The young unemployed

The most pressing problem for young unemployed people, apart from the lack of a job, is a chronic shortage of money. A survey, funded by the Department of Education and Science and published in 1983, found that 60 per cent of the unemployed young people interviewed said they could not manage with the limited amount of money at their disposal.[45] A study of unemployed young people in the West Midlands carried out in 1981 — *before* the most recent cuts — found that 'shortage of money emerged time and again as an obstacle both to social interaction and to finding a satisfactory lifestyle'.[46]

In April 1984 an 18-year-old from Barnsley wrote to CPAG about the cut in her benefit:

> I am 18 and had a drop of £6.20 for two weeks. I can not make up the cut the Tories have made and have to cut back in many ways. My parents only let us pay board and they keep it as low as they can. They don't make me pay for anything else. My parents are not on supplementary and it is a good job as they try to subsidise my loss the best way they can.

Although critics of the government's policies would argue that it is not the job of parents to support their unemployed teenage children financially, there is no doubt that this is indeed what is happening. The survey of youth unemployment in the North-east mentioned above, carried out *before* 18- to 20-year-olds had their benefit cut by £3.10 per week, found that:

> besides much needed moral encouragement, families provided

our sample with substantial financial subsidies. On average, our young people gave their parents £10 per week for their keep. If they are aged 18 or over this leaves them with £13.65 [£11.45 after April 1984] to pay for improving skills, travel to the centres, savings for the future, clothes, drink and cigarettes, discos, concerts, newspapers and cups of coffee to help pass the time. Those under 18 will only be left with £5.80 a week [£6.50 from November 1983] after giving their parents their keep.

Government cuts in young people's benefits have been felt most harshly in families where the parents are badly off but not eligible for or not claiming SB or HB. One working single parent wrote to the *Financial Times* 'to bring to some of your readers the realities of life for the disadvantaged under this government'. Her 19-year-old unemployed son had just had his weekly benefit of £24.55 reduced to £21.45. She pointed out that 'the cut in benefit will affect us both as he will give me less board and lodging and will have less to keep himself'.[47]

The enforced dependence of unemployed teenagers, far from fulfilling the Conservative aim of family unity, can cause considerable family tension. Lack of money means that young people can be stuck at home all day, doing very little. This is hardly a recipe for harmony at a stage in family life — the adjustment of both parent(s) and child to the teenager's impending adulthood—which is anyway notoriously difficult. Contrary to the 'scare stories' mentioned above about young people leaving home to get benefit, most young people are trapped in the parental home by their unemployment.

> At least at home there is a roof, there is family food on which to subsidise yourself, some kind of support from family, friends and familiar surroundings. On £23 [£21.45 for 18- to 20-year-olds] you haven't enough to contribute anything to the family budget nor to lead any kind of social life, so not only is your family faced with having you around all day, they usually have you dismally hanging around in the evening and at weekends as well. Tempers fly, depression and apathy set in and you stay put.[48]

The charity Youthaid reports that a significant cause of youth homelessness is forced parental eviction of teenagers — often accompanied by violence or the threat of violence.[49] According to the Social Security Advisory Committee (SSAC), organisations dealing with homeless young people have reported that quarrels over finance are a significant cause of young people leaving the parental home.[50]

The government policy of cutting the benefits of young people can only create additional tensions between parents and their adolescent children—not a recipe for the happy family life of its ideology. The government's concern that some unemployed people have left home at the state's expense appears to be misplaced. Traditionally, the route to a separate home lay through a job. For many young people, this route is no longer open. Already, the benefit rule changes have drawn a sharp distinction between the dependent unemployed teenager and the 'adult' working teenager deemed capable of contributing a substantial amount to his or her parent(s).

The government's view that young people receive too much benefit to want a job is also not founded in fact. All the evidence is that single people are the least likely to be better off out of work than in work. The DHSS Cohort Study found that only 9 per cent of under-20-year-olds had 'replacement ratios' of 80 per cent and above, and that only 7 per cent of those men in the study who had replacement ratios of 80 per cent or over were under 20.[51] (A 'replacement ratio' is achieved by comparing the level of benefit with the level of wages; so, someone who earns £50, but would receive benefit of £40 has a 'replacement ratio' of 80 per cent.) Nevertheless, a common reaction of parents faced with asking their working children for the substantial sum for rent assumed by the DHSS, as well as money for keep, has been to comment that their children had little incentive to take a low-paid job (see below).

Youth Training Scheme

All reports suggest that the take-up of YTS places has been significantly lower than expected. In February 1984, for example, 442,356 places had been approved,[52] but only 259,282 filled[53]—representing a take-up rate of 59 per cent. No one seems certain about what the young people supposed to be on Youth Training Schemes are actually doing. But, analysing MSC figures, Youthaid came to the conclusion that 'a considerable but unknown number . . . are on the dole rather than the YTS'.[54] There also seems to be a remarkably high drop-out rate, estimated by *Labour Research* at one in four.[55] A sample survey of early leavers found that 38 per cent of those who left had found work, 29 per cent changed their YTS placement and 24 per cent were on the dole.[56] Since December 1983 6,985 young people had their benefit reduced under the '40 per cent rule' (see p 83).[57]

The low take-up of YTS places has put pressure on managing agents in the private sector, who lose money if they do not fill enough of their placements—a pressure that they sometimes pass on. CPAG received information about one West Midlands firm which sent letters to young people in the Knowsley area of

Birmingham (all of whom were claiming benefit whilst studying under the 21-hour rule), inviting them to take up a YTS place. The letters went on to say that their benefit might be affected if they refused a place. The letters were later withdrawn after the matter was raised at the Area Manpower Board of the MSC.

It also appears that careers officers have the names of young people on benefit and will usually supply them quite readily to the managing agents of YTS schemes — though some groups (for instance, in Avon) have refused to do so.[58] Some careers officers have also threatened cuts in benefit in an attempt to make recalcitrant teenagers visit them. In November 1983 the lead story in the *Dudley Express and Star* was 'Town's Lazy Teenagers Shun Work'. The principal careers officer was threatening to report 50 'lazy Dudley school-leavers' to the unemployment benefit office for failing to respond to invitations to discuss YTS courses with the careers staff.[59] Six weeks later, the principal careers officer again used the *Dudley Express*, this time to say that the numbers he intended to report had risen to 109; and that he had recently sent school-leavers a final warning that their weekly benefit would be cut from £16.50 to £9.90 'for not even attempting to explain their disinterest in joining a youth training scheme'.[60]

If young unemployed people are compelled to join a scheme, there is little incentive for the organisers to ensure that the training they give is responsive to participants' needs. Nor does compulsion make for enthusiastic trainees. The Association of British Chambers of Commerce reported recently:

> Chambers considered the proposal that those refusing to take training or work opportunities should be denied unemployment benefit, but there was strong opposition to it. Chambers with highly successful YTS schemes would naturally be disinclined to train reluctant trainees. We therefore consider that other methods of encouragement...should be undertaken.[61]

Despite these strong opinions, uttered by those who actually run many of the YTS schemes, the government appears to have other ideas. Echoing the Prime Minister's sentiment that unemployment should not be an option for the young (see p 90), Lord Young addressed a rhetorical question to the Building Employers' Federation on 4 December last year: 'if we can offer young people good training . . . or a job...why offer anything else? Living off the state does not represent an ideal start in life for a youngster.' It turned out, however, that he was not proposing a massive job creation programme for the young (despite being the minister charged with finding new methods of stimulating employment). Instead, he seemed to be suggesting the complete withdrawal of benefit from those who refused a training place (or, presumably, a job).

The *Financial Times*, in an editorial the morning after Lord Young's speech, treated his suggestion with scepticism: 'It is better that youngsters enter training schemes because they expect to gain from them than because they have no alternative.' With admirable understatement, the paper judged that 'new ideas for reducing youth unemployment are badly needed, but it is doubtful whether Lord Young's suggestion can provide the basis for action.'

The Prime Minister, however, clearly has no such doubts. In an interview with the BBC on 17 December, she repeated her view that 'unemployment ought not to be a choice up to the age of 18 . . . They ought not to be able to leave [school at 16] and go to unemployment.' It is clear that measures to make the payment of benefit for those 16- and 17-year-olds not in school, at work or on a training scheme 'not...a choice' would receive approval from the highest levels of government. Whether young people would welcome this particular manifestation of government concern about youth unemployment levels is another question.

Young workers

The living standards of young people in work have been affected both directly, by the government's attempts to depress youth wages, and indirectly, by the high rent contribution they are now expected to make if they are living at home and their parents are on HB (see p 84).

There is a conspicuous lack of evidence supporting the government's belief that lower wage levels for young people will lead to more jobs. For example, an Institute of Manpower Studies report (commissioned by the Department of Employment) estimated that 94 per cent of jobs under the Young Workers Scheme would have existed anyway.[62] No doubt, if wages for young people were considerably lower than those for older workers, some employers would choose to employ more young people; but the reduction in youth unemployment would merely be achieved at the price of displacing older workers. There is no evidence that lower wages would lead to the creation of a significant number of *new* jobs.

The government's eagerness to allow market forces to dictate the wage levels of young workers, unfettered by other controls such as wages council agreements, also takes no account of the 'market value' of the wage in terms of spending power. As *The Times* said in an editorial: 'Ministers . . . seem reluctant to accept that the remuneration in the low-wage jobs they want young people to take (where such jobs exist) may actually be below the level of subsistence tolerable in a civilised society.'[63] Low wages inevitably restrict the young person's ability to make a life of his/her own away from the parental home. Yet it is wage-earners living with parents who have been singled out to bear the costs of cuts in their parents' HB. By November 1984 an estimated 300,000 young people were affected by the increases in non-dependant deductions.

In defending the cuts in HB for parents with working children, the government argued that a weekly contribution of £8.20 per person was not excessive. It cited the average weekly wages of teenagers: for males aged 18-20 years, £95; for females of the same age, £78.20. For 16- to 17-year-olds (expected to pay £3.10 per week from November 1984), the average weekly male rate is £61, and the average female wage £55.70. Yet no research has been done to establish the wage levels of young people living at home whose parents are on HB, and these levels might well be lower. Average wage levels also disguise the very considerable financial burden placed on low income families whose teenagers are themselves at the bottom end of the wage scale.

The SSAC expressed considerable concern at the lack of information on whether teenagers actually paid the contributions being deducted from their parents' HB.[64] CPAG shared this concern and also wanted to know more about the wage levels of teenagers affected by the government's cuts. Jointly with Youthaid, it decided to ask those people who were likely to be affected. A letter in the *Daily Star* in April 1984 produced 111 replies in four weeks.[65]

What emerged from the letters was that the government had intruded upon a very delicate matter of negotiation in family relations, as both parents and children adjusted to the transition of the latter from childhood to the responsibilities of adulthood. Many parents were very protective of their children's right to enjoy their new wages, and were reluctant to demand more for rent and keep than they had already fixed themselves. This was the case even though the majority of correspondents were on low incomes—including 67 on SB. Other parents were frightened that their children would leave home if they demanded more money. One parent on SB wrote: 'As my boys are on a low wage I could not possibly ask them for any more money. I am scared they may leave and that's the last thing I want to happen.'

In dismissing the concern of the SSAC—that the increases in non-dependant deductions had 'gone beyond what is fair and reasonable'—the Secretary of State for Social Services argued: 'The increases could only be described as "losses" if there was a failure by a working adult to meet his share of housing costs, and it is not the role of a benefit scheme financed by the taxpayer to shield households from the consequences of such failure.'[66]

The consequences of the government's policy have been not only greater deprivation for the families involved, but also rent arrears. The local authority associations reported to the SSAC that rent arrears arising from the non-dependant deductions cause them a significant problem.[67] One parent wrote to CPAG:

> I have just received an eviction order for £54 because I cannot afford the £8.20 a week. It was slapped on me out of the blue. I did not realise that my rent would change because my son found a job. He is now talking about leaving home so that I don't have to pay. I think it is sickening. I have told him to go on the dole [where, because her son was 18, no deduction would be made] ... but he likes his job.

The present punitive levels of non-dependant deduction evoke memories of the 1930s. As Youthaid's director Paul Lewis commented: 'We do not just have the unemployment of the 1930s, we are getting the hated family means test too.'[68]

Studying on the dole

As shown earlier in this chapter, the history of the rules governing part-time study whilst on benefit is a classic example of the DHSS's attempts to contain what it sees as a problem — the burgeoning numbers of claimants — by administrative means. It appears that the DHSS had also acted without any consultation with the Department of Education and Science (DES), which simultaneously was examining how colleges could be opened up to the unemployed. A DES-funded report from Youthaid found that the rules for getting benefit whilst studying were widely misunderstood and misinterpreted by both the DHSS and colleges.[69] They were so complex that educators saw the issue of benefit whilst studying as a problem rather than as an opportunity.

The DHSS's measures have had ridiculous consequences—unemployed youngsters could find their benefit stopped because they were studying too hard by doing too much homework. A complaint frequently made to CPAG by puzzled and confused teenagers and parents has been that whilst the government seemed happy to pay young unemployed people to kick their heels at home doing nothing, it put every obstacle in their way if they wanted to fill their time usefully by improving their job qualifications.

This has highlighted the different financial provisions for young people of the same age. Eighteen-year-olds continuing their schooling are regarded as child dependants of their parents, who therefore qualify for child benefit. Young people of the same age who are unemployed, however, can qualify for benefit in their own right. CPAG and others have argued that the first group should also be paid an income as of right, thus giving teenagers an incentive to stay on in education.[70] There are certainly fears, though, that the government or the reviews could propose equality in the other direction, ie, by putting unemployed 16- to 18-year-olds in the same position as those still at school.

Conclusion

The prevailing Conservative ideology and the renewed pressure for further reductions in public spending suggest that young people's benefits may continue to be a target for yet greater cuts. Record jobless levels in September 1984[71] have also given added impetus to the Chancellor's moves to keep wage rates down, particularly for the young.

There are, however, serious contradictions between the declared aims of the government in cutting benefits and depressing youth wages, and the actual consequences. Thus, according to leaked documents, the Cabinet's Family Policy Group considered 'methods of developing children into self-reliant, capable, enterprising and fulfilled adults'. Yet, in cutting the benefits of the young unemployed, the government has made them more dependent on their parents, not less.

However, it would seem that the government can count on agreement from some quarters for its views on parental responsibility. In the words of Parry Rogers, one of the three people carrying out the review on benefits for children and young people, 'If as a parent, you bring children into the world, you take on a responsibility for those children up to a certain point.'[72] Quite what that point is, is a matter of debate, as the whole issue of young unemployed people at college has brought into focus. 'Parental influence' is clearly seen by Conservatives as including an element of financial control. Give a teenager too much money and, in the words of Parry Rogers, it makes him/her 'a good deal less susceptible to parental influence, [and] to the family environment, than in the present situation'.[73]

Popular feeling against the government's attitudes to young people has yet to be mobilised. Between 500,000 and 600,000 young people under 20 are now unemployed;[74] many more are in low-paid work. The effects of further attempts to depress both wages and benefits will be felt by families across a wide social spectrum, including Conservative voters. It remains to be seen whether any further moves to shift financial responsibility on to families will finally compel a reaction.

References

1 Schedule 2, para 6, Social Security Act 1980; Reg 11, Supplementary Benefit (Conditions of Entitlement) Regulations 1980, No 1586.
2 Lynda Chalker, Social Security Bill, Committee Stage, 19 February 1980, cols 892 and 893.

3 £3m was the estimate given for the abolition of SB for school-leavers in the financial year 1979/80 by *Social Assistance: a review of the supplementary benefits scheme in Great Britain*, DHSS July 1978, para 4.8.
4 Schedule 2, para 30, Social Security Act 1980; Reg 3, Supplementary Benefit (Aggregation) Regulations 1980, No 982.
5 Child Benefit (General) Amendment Regulations 1980, No 470.
6 Reg 3(6), 3(7) and 3(9), Supplementary Benefit (Requirements and Resources) Amendment Regulations 1984, No 1102; Reg 4(5), Supplementary Benefit (Miscellaneous Amendments) Regulations 1984.
7 Reg 2(7), Supplementary Benefit (Housing Benefits)(Requirements and Resources) Consequential Amendment Regulations 1983, No 505.
8 See, for example, Hugh Rossi, *House of Commons Hansard*, 30 June 1982, cols 328-9W: 'But as a corollary for the decisions to abolish deductions [from housing benefit] in respect of non-dependants aged 16 or 17 the supplementary benefit housing addition will be withdrawn from 16 and 17 year old non-householders.'
9 See *Statement by the Secretary of State for Social Services in response to the Report of the Social Security Advisory Committee on the Housing Benefits Amendment Regulations 1984, the Housing Benefits Amendment Regulations 1984, the Housing Benefits Amendment (No 2) Regulations 1984 and the Draft Supplementary Benefit (Requirements) Amendment Regulations 1984*, para 23, HMSO February 1984, Cmnd 9155.
10 Reg 4, Supplementary Benefit (Requirements) Amendment Regulations 1984, No 282.
11 Youthaid, 'Proof of oral evidence to the review of benefits for children and young people', September 1984.
12 *A New Training Initiative: a programme for action*, HMSO, Cmnd 8455.
13 See Section 20, Social Security Act 1975.
14 S87(2), National Insurance Act 1911.
15 Youthaid, *YTS Briefing*, 1984.
16 *The Economist*, 7 January 1984.
17 Reg 7, Supplementary Benefit (Conditions of Entitlement) Regulations 1980, No 1586.
18 See Tony Newton, *House of Commons Hansard*, 27 July 1982, col 18: 'As Hon Members know, there was much anxiety earlier in the year...when it emerged that under the previous understanding of the regulations up to 21 hours' classroom instruction were permitted. The result was that youngsters taking full sixth-form-type courses of two to three A-levels could in some circumstances qualify for benefit. This had never been the intention... The outcome was the memorandum issued in March which advised that time spent in lunch breaks and private study should be counted in the 21-hour limit.'
19 RSB 26/82.
20 Introduced by the Supplementary Benefit (Miscellaneous Amendments) Regulations 1982, No 907.
21 See *Report by the Social Security Advisory Committee on the draft Supplementary Benefits (Miscellaneous Amendment) Regulations 1982*, HMSO July 1982, Cmnd 8598.
22 Tony Newton, *House of Commons Hansard*, 23 July 1982, cols 329-30W.
23 CF 38/83.
24 DHSS Circular, S21/84.
25 Introduced by the Supplementary Benefit (Miscellaneous Amendments) Regulations 1983, No 938.
26 *The Economist*, 27 August 1983.
27 *Guardian*, 28 August 1983.
28 *The Times*, 30 August 1983.

29 *Guardian*, 19 February 1983.
30 *Guardian*, 17 February 1983.
31 *Statement by the Secretary of State for Social Services, in response to the report by the Social Security Advisory Committee on the proposed withdrawal of the non-householders' rent contribution from 18-20-year-olds*, HMSO February 1984, Cmnd 9155.
32 *Daily Telegraph*, 25 May 1984.
33 *The Times*, 3 April 1984.
34 Under Reg 9, Supplementary Benefit Requirements Regulations 1983, No 1399.
35 *Sunday Times*, 21 August 1983.
36 Rhodes Boyson, *House of Commons Hansard*, 10 May 1984, col 1190.
37 Margaret Thatcher, House of Commons, 27 July 1981.
38 W Wells, 'The Relative Pay and Employment of Young People', Department of Employment Research Paper 42.
39 *Observer*, 31 September 1984.
40 *Daily Express*, 15 June 1983.
41 *The Times*, 22 August 1983.
42 *The Times*, 30 August 1983.
43 *New Society*, 2 June 1983.
44 *Financial Times*, 31 March 1983.
45 Department of Education and Science, *Young People in the 80s: a survey*, HMSO 1983.
46 'Growing Up Without Work: two case studies', European Centre for Work and Society June 1983.
47 *Financial Times*, 3 April 1984.
48 *Guardian*, 24 August 1984.
49 Youthaid, 'Youth Unemployment: a background paper', December 1983.
50 *Report of the Social Security Advisory Committee on the draft Housing Benefit Amendments*, HMSO February 1984, Cmnd 9150.
51 DHSS Cohort Study of Unemployed Men, Working Papers, DHSS 1982.
52 Manpower Services Commission figures quoted in *Labour Research*, May 1984.
53 *House of Commons Hansard*, 28 March 1984, col 199.
54 Youthaid, 'Youth Training Scheme: numbers and cost', 12 June 1984.
55 *Labour Research*, May 1984.
56 See note 53 above.
57 *House of Commons Hansard*, 3 July 1984, col 140.
58 Investigation by David Bull, Bristol University.
59 *Dudley Express and Star*, 28 November 1983.
60 *Dudley Express and Star*, 18 January 1984.
61 ABCC, 'Curbing Leviathan', June 1984.
62 *New Statesman*, 6 January 1984.
63 *The Times*, 30 August 1983.
64 See note 50 above.
65 For full details, see Shirley Cusack and Jo Roll, *Families Rent Apart*, CPAG 1985.
66 *Statement by the Secretary of State for Social Services, in response to the SSAC report on the Housing Benefit Amendments 1984*, para 17, HMSO, Cmnd 9155.
67 *Report by the Social Security Advisory Committee on the draft Housing Benefit Regulations 1984*, para 29, HMSO February 1984, Cmnd 9150.
68 *Youthaid News*, December 1984.
69 Youthaid, *Studying on the Dole*, 1984.
70 See Louie Burghes and Ray Stagles, *No Choice at 16: a study of educational maintenance allowances*, CPAG 1983.

71 The September figures showed a record 13.6 per cent unemployment rate nationally, with higher figures regionally. For example, 19.1 per cent in the North and 21.9 per cent in Northern Ireland.
72 Comments by Parry Rogers in the course of oral evidence being given by Youthaid, 13 August 1984, official transcript.
73 As note 72.
74 According to *Employment Gazette* figures, youth unemployment has fluctuated between these levels during the last year.

8. Tried and found wanting: **the take-up of means-tested benefits**

JONATHAN BRADSHAW

One facet of the crisis within the Department of Health and Social Security (DHSS) that is described in this book is the fact that many people are not receiving the means-tested benefits they are entitled to. This can partly be attributed to the sheer complexity and extent of the system—a complexity which has been seized on recently by some people, such as the Institute for Fiscal Studies (IFS)[1] and the National Council of Voluntary Organisations,[2] and used in different ways to justify their proposals for radical reforms of the social security system.

Some of those who seek to reform social security wish to do so by extending the amount of means-testing. The IFS, for example, has called for 'a savage but selective retrenchment of the benefits system'.[3] It is, therefore, appropriate to look again at the whole question of the take-up of benefits, both in the context of the current crisis within the DHSS and in the context of the reforms suggested. Even though this is a well-worked theme, the facts and the effects of low take-up are important to the current debate and bear repeating.

There are very powerful pressures for extending the means-testing of benefits. Means-testing, it is said, enables help to be concentrated on those who need it most. By restricting help to only the most needy, more help can be given to them, whilst still allowing public expenditure (and thus taxation) to be cut. Standing against these arguments are the three fundamental defects of means-tested benefits:

- that they are complicated and expensive to administer;
- that many of those eligible do not claim them; and
- that they exacerbate the poverty trap (see p 54).

Much of the rest of this book, and in particular Chapters 3 and 9, examine the complications of administering the current means-tested system. This chapter, however, will look at one of the other problems: that of low take-up.

The extent and value of non-take-up

The research evidence on the level and causes of non-take-up was reviewed by A Deacon and J Bradshaw in 1983.[4] There is no single source of estimates of take-up. Official estimates tend to emerge haphazardly in answers to parliamentary questions, in reports of government surveys and in statistical reports. CPAG's recent leaflet provides a useful and up-to-date review of current evidence.[5]

Supplementary benefit

The most important means-tested benefit is supplementary benefit (SB). Official estimates of take-up are based on an analysis of the Family Expenditure Survey (FES) which is carried out every two years by statisticians in the DHSS. The estimates are always considerably out of date—the latest are for 1981 and did not emerge until November 1983. Thus, the next estimates (for 1983) will not appear until November 1985.

It would appear that one of the reasons that led the government to decide in 1979 to analyse the FES only bi-annually in future was that changes from year to year were too small to justify the annual analysis. But since 1979 the number of people on SB has been increasing very rapidly. This is partly as a result of changes in policy, such as the abolition of earnings-related supplement and the 'abatement' of (ie, cuts in) short-term benefits. More importantly, it is because of the massive increase in the number of long-term unemployed people eligible for SB. This has had a marked impact on the amount of unclaimed benefits. In 1979 70 per cent of those eligible for SB were claiming it, and the estimated benefit unclaimed was £355m.[6] By 1981 take-up was more or less the same, at 71 per cent; but the value of unclaimed benefits had more than doubled, to £760m.[7] The number of pensioners, sick and disabled people and one-parent families who were eligible non-claimants actually fell between 1979 and 1981. *All* of the increase in the numbers and amounts of unclaimed benefit came from the increase in the numbers of unemployed people eligible for SB. As can be seen in Table 1, the unemployed had the highest level per person of unclaimed entitlement to SB.

Since 1981 the number of people unemployed, particularly long term, has continued to rise, and the numbers eligible for SB have increased by over a million between 1981 and 1983. A fairly crude estimate of the take-up situation in 1983 can be produced by extrapolating from the number of households in receipt of SB in August 1983 (the latest period for which data are available). Table 2 shows that the number of unemployed people who were eligible for SB but not claiming it may have increased by 235,000, and the

Table 1: *Estimates of take-up of SB for 1981*

	Total entitled (000s)	*Proportion receiving (%)*	*Estimated benefit unclaimed (£m pa)*	*Average weekly amount unclaimed (£)*
Pensioners	2,480	67	210	5.00
Sick and disabled	290	67	70	14.30
Unemployed	1,580	75	410	19.60
One-parent families	400	88	40	15.30
Total	*4,820*	*71*	*760*	*10.50*

Source: House of Commons Hansard, 30 November 1983, cols 539-40.

Table 2: *Estimates of take-up of SB (including certificated housing benefit) for 1983*

	Nos in receipt (000s)	*Nos eligible and not in receipt (000s)*	*Average weekly amount unclaimed (£)*	*Estimated benefit unclaimed (£m pa)*
Pensioners	1,600	790	5.66	233
Sick and disabled	200	99	16.28	84
Unemployed	1,900	630	22.19	730
One-parent families	430	59	17.32	53
Other	170	57	20.50	61
Total	*4,300*	*1,640*	*13.61*	*1,161*

Source: Extrapolated from (1) numbers in receipt of SB in August 1983; (2) the proportion of each group receiving SB in 1981, and (3) average weekly amount unclaimed in 1981 for each group uprated by the price index July 1981 to July 1983.

total annual amount of unclaimed benefit may have risen to £1,161m per year, by 1983.

Over the years, a good deal of work has been done on the problems of estimating the take-up of SB and analysing the characteristics of non-claimants, including a paper published by the DHSS in 1978 on the take-up of SB.[8] More recently, a paper was prepared for the Social Services Select Committee, based on an analysis of the 1979 FES and the 1978/79 Family Finances Survey.[9] This concluded that about three-quarters of non-pensioners with a high level of unclaimed entitlement were either living in reasonably well-off households or were claimants where either the 'head' or the wife had been away from work for less than five weeks. Among pensioners, about a fifth lived in wider households (who would have other sources of income). There was no evidence that having capital balances was an explanation for non-take-up in either group.

These estimates, based on the FES, cover 'primary' take-up of the basic weekly benefit (which, since 1981, has been calculated to include those with an automatic entitlement to extra weekly benefit for fuel). However, we have to look elsewhere for estimates of 'secondary' take-up—that is, the take-up of additional requirements (extra weekly benefit) and single payments (lump-sum grants) by those already in receipt of SB. The best source on 'secondary' take-up is the research carried out by R Berthoud in 1982.[10] He found that while most people entitled to additional requirements for heating were receiving them, only one-third of those entitled to other special extra allowances actually got them. He also discovered that unclaimed entitlement to single payments was worth about £80 per claimant—about three times the amount normally received in a year in single payments.

Housing benefit

There are no estimates of the take-up of housing benefit (HB) yet available; instead, we have to rely on estimates of the take-up of housing rebates, for 1982. The figures given in Table 3 are derived from similar sources to those for the take-up of SB, but employ slightly different methods.

Table 3: *Take-up of housing rebates 1982 (%)*

	Proportion eligible receiving		
	Rent rebates	*Rent allowances*	*Rate rebates*
Pensioner households	89	80	81
Non-pensioner households	59	33	47
Households with dependent children	58	33	45
All households	*72*	*62*	*65*

Source: House of Commons Hansard, 6 March 1984, cols 565-6.

The take-up figures for rent rebates and allowances and rate rebates should provide a good estimate of the take-up of HB. HB could have led to a net increase in the take-up of rent rebates (standard HB), but only for those who were formerly in receipt of SB (certificated HB). Table 3 shows that the take-up of housing rebates was considerably lower among non-pensioner households, in particular families with children, than among pensioner households.

There are also no up-to-date official estimates of the amounts unclaimed in housing rebates. However, it is possible to derive a crude estimate from data on expenditure on housing rebates, and an estimate of unclaimed benefit in 1983/84 is given in Table 4.

Table 4: *Estimates of housing rebates unclaimed: 1983/4*

	Take-up	*Nos eligible not claiming (000s)*	*Average weekly amount unclaimed*	*Amount unclaimed (£m)*
Rent rebates	72	672	£7.93	277
Rent allowances	62	184	£8.85	85
Rate rebates	65	2,052	£2.70	288
Total				*650*

Source: Calculated from data in *House of Commons Hansard*, 19 March 1984, col 372.

This estimate assumes that the average amount unclaimed is the same as the average amount claimed. Bradshaw and Beadham[12] found that, on average, eligible non-claimants would have qualified for smaller rebates than those claiming, partly because of higher take-up and higher eligibility among single parents. However, non-claimant couples were entitled to similar amounts to those receiving. Given that take-up is lower among families with children than pensioners, and that families with children are likely to have higher rents (and, therefore, higher rebates) than pensioners, it is not unreasonable to assume that the amount of rebate foregone is equivalent to that received.

Family income supplement

Compared with SB and HB, family income supplement (FIS) is available to far fewer people. However, it is important in debates about means-testing because it is the kind of simple means-tested system of child support that those who advocate selectivity would like to see replacing universal child benefit. It also appears to have a particularly low level of take-up. The official estimate for FIS take-up is still that derived from the Family Finances Survey (FFS) in 1978/79—about 51 per cent.[13] Since then, the number of families in receipt of FIS has more than doubled,[14] which could indicate an improvement in take-up. However, during the same period there have been other changes—such as real improvements in the prescribed limits, changes in the hours rules for single parents, a sharp decline in the demand for labour, and reduced opportunities for overtime and second earners—which will all have led to increases in the numbers eligible.

In mid-1983 about 190,000 families were receiving FIS — on average, £12 per week.[15] If take-up was still 51 per cent, then 183,000 families were eligible non-claimants. In 1978/79 it was estimated that non-claimants of FIS were, on average, eligible for about three-quarters of the amount of those claiming. Therefore, the amount unclaimed in FIS in 1983 might have been about £86m (183,000 x £9 x 52).

The impact of non-take-up

It is possible to combine the estimates in the foregoing pages to produce an overall estimate of the money foregone by those not claiming means-tested benefits.

Table 5: *Estimate of the take-up of the principal means-tested benefits 1983 (Great Britain)*

	Take-up rate %	*Nos eligible not claiming (000)*	*Average weekly amount unclaimed*	*Annual total unclaimed (£m)*
SB[1]	72	1,640	£13.60	1,161
FIS	51	183	£9.00[2]	86
Standard HB				
rent rebates[3]	72	672	£7.93	277
rent allowances[3]	62	184	£8.85	85
rate rebates[3]	65	2,052	£2.70	288
Free school meals	70	461	£1.95	47
Total				*1,944*

Notes: 1. including certificated HB; 2. three-quarters of average claimed; and 3. see Table 4.

The total of nearly £2,000m in Table 5 can only be a very approximate figure. Nevertheless, it provides an indication of the huge sums of money that are being lost by poor people who fail to claim means-tested benefits. How much an individual family will lose by failing to claim benefits will, of course, depend on the circumstances — single parents failing to claim SB will lose considerably more than pensioners failing to claim a small supplementary addition to their basic national insurance pension.

It is possible to simulate what standard types of household may fail to claim in means-tested benefits; and there are many examples in the welfare rights literature of huge sums foregone by individual claimants. However, there have been few attempts to assess the effects of non-take-up on the income of samples of families. One exception is work by J Millar,[16] who analysed the FFS to assess the value of unclaimed benefits to low income families. She found that 64 per cent of lone parents and 39 per cent of two-parent families in the sample had some unclaimed entitlement to means-tested benefits. For a fifth of the lone parents and half of the two-parent families, this amounted to not more than 5 per cent of their net weekly incomes. However, another one in seven of the lone parents and one in ten of the two-parent families were entitled to benefits equivalent to at least half as much again as their current net incomes. Millar also calculated the extent to which the numbers of families living below the SB poverty line would have been reduced if they had claimed their full entitlement to means-tested benefits. If the lone parents had claimed their entitlement, the number living below SB level income would have halved; and if the two-parent families had done likewise, the number living below SB level income would have fallen by a third.

Encouragement of take-up

In the past, all governments, perhaps particularly Conservative governments, have made considerable efforts to make means tests work. At present, 8 per cent of all government expenditure on advertising is spent by the DHSS. About £3m was spent on health and social security related press and TV advertising in 1983—and a good deal of that went on marketing means-tested benefits. Between 1979/80 and 1983/84, the DHSS spent £98,000 on advertising SB, £1.6m on FIS and £760,000 on HB. These are trivial amounts compared with the level of expenditure on benefits; but they do indicate that the government is not entirely unconcerned about the problem of take-up.[17]

Apart from this continuing programme to advertise benefits, some efforts are made to make forms more widely available and easier to understand. Claim forms for SB are now issued to all pensioners and widows, all unemployed claimants and all sickness benefit claimants. In December 1982 the postal claim form for SB was introduced for unemployed people, and it is now being tried for pensioners and other groups of claimants. It is too early to tell whether this has had any impact on take-up. Reducing the number of claimants who have to attend overstretched offices must have encouraged some to claim who otherwise might not have done so. The DHSS has also collaborated in many of the take-up exercises mounted by local authorities. It has itself also launched a number of specific attempts to improve take-up, including the Freefone schemes in most regions and the use of benefit buses. The Scottish Region of the DHSS, in conjunction with Strathclyde welfare rights officers, has undertaken a special campaign to improve the take-up of benefits among the physically and mentally handicapped, with dramatic results.

The fact that means-tested benefits fail to reach many low income households is not a matter that concerns the Institute of Directors, however. They told the review of benefits for children and young people: 'Some think the low take-up rates a weakness of the present system; we think them a strength. First, a low take-up saves large amounts of government spending. Second, it is in substantial measure the result of self selection among the potential users of the welfare system.'[18] No government has ever adopted that view.

The future of means-testing

The IFS is just one, and perhaps the most authoritative, of a growing number of new advocates of means tests. It proposes that child benefit and pensions should become wholly means-tested, and hopes to overcome the problem of take-up by new technology. Taxes and benefits would be fixed annually on the basis of a return of income. Anyone who submits a return would be issued with a computerised card.

> All tax payers would be required to make an annual return of income to the Inland Revenue. . . Anyone else could submit a return and people who would be entitled to benefit but who are not liable for tax would clearly find it advantageous to do so. We do not, however, envisage that compulsion would extend beyond those liable for tax, and to this extent potential beneficiaries could escape the net, and some problems of take up would remain. Unless we are prepared to imprison confused old ladies for failing to claim rebates, there is no income transfer mechanism which can escape this problem.[19]

It also argues that the unpopularity of means tests is:

> purely instinctive . . . about form rather than substance . . . superficial sloganising. . .
>
> What is offensive are specific and potentially humiliating enquiries into the affairs of poor households which discriminate between them and the population as a whole. The intention of the proposals is to effect a considerable reduction in these enquiries by utilising much more extensive information which is, or could be, collected through the tax system.[20]

It is being argued that the complications of means-testing can be overcome by technology, and that the problem of take-up will largely be overcome in the same way. In the IFS scheme, benefit would be based on current weekly income, and over- and underpayments would be dealt with by an end of year assessment based on the annual tax return.

In practice, however, it is doubtful whether a scheme could be operated so simply. There is a limit to which people on low income could carry an under-payment until the end of the year. And it is difficult to believe that the proposed method of recovering over-payments of benefit will not further complicate the scheme. Apart from income changes, the system would need to deal with changes in circumstances as they occur during the year — changes in the employment status of both husband and wife, changes in housing costs, births and deaths, marriages and divorces, young people starting work and leaving home and so on. Two means-tested benefits — HB and SB — are already breaking under the strain of dealing with some of these changes on a weekly basis; and FIS, also means-tested, only survives as a viable benefit by ignoring any changes in circumstances that occur for a year after benefit is received. The social security system as a whole survives because most pensioners, most sick and disabled people and a substantial minority of unemployed people receive national insurance benefits, which are not subject to a test of means, and do not call for detailed reassessment at every change in circumstances.

Even if these problems of administration and take-up can be overcome by the use of technology, and even if Whitehall is capable of the massive reorganisation of the Inland Revenue and social security administration necessary to establish an integrated tax and benefit system, there remains the poverty trap (see p 54). Under the IFS scheme, the very high notional 'marginal tax rates' of the present system will be replaced by actual marginal tax rates which are only slightly lower and which affect a much larger number of families.

Conclusion

In the light of these arguments, any proposal to extend means testing must be subject to very careful scrutiny. It appears that the IFS authors have misunderstood the real nature of the problem of take-up. People do not take up means-tested benefits to which they are entitled for a variety of reasons. Certainly, 'humiliating enquiries' and their discriminatory nature play a part in deterring applications — but there are a host of other, possibly more important, reasons to do with the inevitable complexity of means-tested benefits. Non-take-up is not just about 'superficial sloganising', nor is it merely the plight of confused old ladies failing to claim rebates. It is an apparently intractable by-product of delivering benefits according to means. It is also a very large problem indeed.

Non-take-up causes unnecessary hardship to many poor families.

For certain parts of the country with high concentrations of claimants, it must even be damaging the local economy — those millions of pounds of unclaimed benefit would be spent on stimulating local trade and services. This is perhaps one good reason why local authorities, even in rural areas, are becoming actively involved in increasing the take-up of benefits.

Yet we have allowed dependence on means-tested benefits to grow at a rapid rate in recent years. Either we assume that a formal legal entitlement to benefit means that benefit is in fact delivered; or we have learned to live with the fact that means-tested benefits in Britain are failing to reach so many of those who need them. In either case, the economic interests of the better-off — which would be challenged by more substantive benefit rights not reliant on means-testing — are protected. Those people who are proposing an extension of means-testing as a method of limiting public expenditure further must explain exactly how their schemes are going to operate more successfully than existing means-tested benefits. They must show that, in practice, they will offer more than just another list of rights to benefits in the abstract only.

References

1 A W Dilnot, J A Kay and C N Morris, *The Reform of Social Security*, Institute for Fiscal Studies/Clarendon Press 1984.
2 P Ashby, *Social Security after Beveridge: what next?*, Bedford Square Press 1984.
3 See note 1 above, p 5.
4 A Deacon and J Bradshaw, *Reserved for the Poor: the means test in British social policy*, Basil Blackwell and Martin Robertson 1983.
5 CPAG leaflet on 'Benefits take-up', 1984.
6 See note 4 above.
7 *House of Commons Hansard*, 30 November 1983, cols 539-40.
8 DHSS, *Take-up of Supplementary Benefits*, HMSO 1978.
9 DHSS, 'Take-up of Supplementary Benefits: characteristics of non-claimants', Paper for the Social Services Select Committee (mimeo), 1983.
10 R Berthoud, *The Reform of Supplementary Benefit*, Policy Studies Institute 1984.
11 J R Bradshaw and R Beadham, 'Housing rebates: their take-up by families with children', *Poverty 57*, CPAG 1984.
12 As note 11 above.
13 DHSS, *Social Security Statistics, 1983*, HMSO 1983.
14 As note 13 above.
15 As note 13 above.
16 J Millar, 'Non take-up of benefits: the effect on the incomes of families with children', Social Policy Research Unit Working Paper 191, 1984.
17 *House of Commons Hansard*, 1 August 1984, col 355.
18 Institute of Directors, 'Submission to the Review of Benefits for Children and Young People' (mimeo), 1984.
19 See note 1 above, pp 102-3.
20 See note 1 above, p 117.

9. Who's fiddling?
fraud and abuse

ROGER SMITH

As suggested in the Preface (p vii), policy and practice on activating the take-up of rightful entitlement to benefits and on preventing the take-up of wrongful entitlement ('fraud and abuse') can be seen as two sides of the same coin. This chapter explores recent policy and practice on fraud and abuse. It suggests that the government's overemphasis on fraud has worked against other goals which should have been of greater concern to Department of Health and Social Security (DHSS) ministers, such as proper administrative procedures and improved take-up (see Chapters 3 and 8). The simultaneous emphasis on cost-cutting has also led to the distortion of techniques to combat fraud, in frantic efforts to meet the demand to produce identifiable 'weekly benefit savings'. The benefit savings on paper are trotted out to still public concern about fraud, just as benefit entitlement, on paper, stills public anxiety about protecting the needy. In neither case does the reality match the boasts.

The emphasis on fraud

Official concern with fraud is not new. From the mid-1970s Conservative MP Iain Sproat deluged the press and parliament with alleged examples of benefit abuse. His campaign was helped on its way by the conviction of 'King Fiddler' Derek Deevey, who, using 41 aliases, obtained over £36,000 in benefit. Stan Orme, then Labour Secretary of State for Social Services, bowed to the pressures. He established a co-ordinating committee on abuse which produced two reports (one in December 1977 and one in January 1979); and he drew up a 'six-point fraud action plan' with a commitment to resources, training and facilities, improved investigative procedures, new anti-fraud measures, managerial involvement and greater emphasis on fraud awareness.

In announcing this plan, the DHSS pointed to the rising prosecution rate as an indicator of the success it was already having with its anti-fraud activities.

> Social security fraud prosecutions for 1978 are expected to be up by about 16% over 1977 ... the final 1978 figure of fraud prosecutions might not be far short of 30,000—an increase of around 90% since 1975. But...there is no reason to believe that there has been a comparative increase in the amount of underlying fraud. Rather, it is reasonable to conclude that the figures are a measure of the increased efforts staff are putting into anti-fraud work, and of its growing effectiveness.[1]

Figures for convictions in the courts certainly had risen dramatically—from 15,006 in 1975 to 28,575 in 1978.[2] At the same time, however, Stan Orme did say that although 'prosecutions will always be with us . . . for the future . . . we must concentrate on prevention as the main weapon in our armoury'.[3] Here, at least, was an admission that some fraud was preventable given proper administrative procedures in the DHSS. Since then, it appears that ministers have lost sight of this fact altogether.

Most attention on fraud within the social security system is paid to supplementary benefit (SB). There is nothing wrong, of course, with a department responsible for the payment of some £6 billion in SB each year being concerned that it goes only to those entitled. And, given the size of the undertaking, fraud and abuse are bound to occur—just as a degree of shoplifting is anticipated by any large department store. But the ways in which they are controlled need examining from several points of view.

The first is a question of balance. Is the emphasis on fraud correct, compared with that on (to take an obvious example) take-up? Second, there is the issue of administration. Can a concern with fraud become a substitute for proper administrative procedures? If the system was administered better, would there be less opportunity for fraud? Third, 'fraud' is used as a catch-all phrase for activity ranging from organised crime—including, say, the theft of a consignment of order books—to a single parent not reporting casual earnings because of the disruptive effect she knows this will have on her benefit. Are the control systems able to distinguish between these activities and respond accordingly? Fourth, there is the question of civil liberties. Do the methods used in anti-fraud work respect the rights of the subject to due process of law? The claimant, like any other member of society, is entitled to these rights, and their erosion in this field is as serious as in any other.

Lastly, there is the key question of whether or not public emphasis on the fraud work of the DHSS deters prospective claimants. Two points of view are held on this. One is that myths about widespread fraud deter people from applying for benefits, because all claimants are tarred with the same brush and the stigma of claiming is intensified. The other is that by driving away the 'scroungers', an atmosphere is created in which 'honest' people will feel more able to claim.

The 1980 measures

On this last question, Reg Prentice, Conservative social security minister in 1980, appears to have held both views at different times. In February 1980, the month in which plans for the DHSS to step up its anti-fraud work were announced, in line with the Conservatives' manifesto, *Tribune* mischievously quoted from a speech Prentice had made some 10 years previously:

> The myth about widespread abuse is perpetuated by some of the most reactionary newspapers in the country and is used by the Tories for party reasons. Apart from the damage done in general, awful damage is done to individual people in need, because these myths help to create among some people . . . the sense that there is something shameful about applying for benefits to which they are entitled.[4]

However, on 13 February 1980, when the DHSS announced the details of its major drive against fraud, 'voluntary' unemployment and 'liable relatives' (see p 117), it explained in its press release that:

> Mr Prentice stressed that a major aim in this drive is to make a sharp distinction between the 'scrounger' and the genuine claimant, and so create a better atmosphere in which people will not be inhibited from claiming their benefit.[5]

The plan was to 'employ over 1,000 extra specialists, who are expected to save over £50m of taxpayers' money which would otherwise be lost in 1980-81'.

A less public change made at the same time was to move away from an emphasis on prosecution as an indicator of the success of anti-fraud work. Instead, greater stress was laid on the repayment by claimants of 'overpaid' benefit (benefit which they had received over and above their correct entitlement) and on the calculation of projected savings from fraud activity. As a memorandum submitted to the House of Commons was to put it:

> DHSS have been concerned about the costs of prosecuting alleged fraudulent claimants and that the low level of fines imposed was unlikely to deter the professional wrongdoer. Therefore, in 1980, Treasury agreed on a trial basis that DHSS should give priority to maximising savings through stopping unjustified benefits payments with less resources devoted to prosecutions. In consequence the number of detected frauds

resulting in prosecutions have fallen from over 30,000 in 1980-81 to under 26,000 in 1981-2.[6]

The DHSS was, in effect, introducing 'cost criteria'. As a result of this change in emphasis, DHSS prosecutions for SB fraud have declined spectacularly: in 1980/81 they stood at 20,105; by 1982/83 this figure had dropped to 13,589, and by 1983/84 there were only 9,101 prosecutions.[7]

The departmental guidance for fraud officers, the 'Fraud Investigators Guide' (FIG) was altered to reflect the increased weight given to saving money.[8] FIG referred to the formation of 'special exercise teams', with the aim 'of deterring false claims to benefit and of encouraging any person wrongly claiming benefit to withdraw his or her claim' (foreshadowing the techniques of Specialist Claims Control teams — see below, pp 118-23). The emphasis throughout was upon 'cost-effectiveness' at every point of an investigation. FIG accepted that there would be many cases where proof of fraudulent activity was difficult or impossible. New weight was therefore given to the 'non-prosecution' interview, carried out when there was insufficient evidence to substantiate withdrawal of benefit, let alone prosecution. FIG counselled:

> It may be worth interviewing the person and putting to him your reasons for suspecting that he is committing fraud, and asking for his comments. He may give you sufficient information to justify withdrawing (or reducing) his benefit. Or he may decide to withdraw his claim.

So, the target was set; the means established. Now, the scramble was on. Reg Prentice had said that there was £50m worth of fraud to be found in the system. On 6 May 1981, Secretary of State Patrick Jenkin was able to announce that, lo and behold, in the financial year 1980/81 some £50m had been found.[9] A detailed statement (see below) set out the results. The vagaries of day-to-day operations had increased the additional staff complement to 1,225 (from 1,050); whereas rounding the figures in the table below altered the savings figure to £38m from the £40.3m figure mentioned in the Secretary of State's statement. A certain sleight of hand was required to meet the £50m total predicted in February 1980:

> The process of deploying the additional staff of 1050 to fraud and abuse work began in Autumn 1979 and was phased over a number of months. During this preliminary period, which falls within the financial year 1979/80, the savings in benefit payments, as a result of their work, amounted to £13m.[10]

Hence, the apparent total could be increased to £53m.

	Existing staff	*Total with increased staff*	*Savings*		
			By existing staff £m	*By the increased staff £m*	*Increase %*
Unemployment review (SB)	447	906	22	44	100
Unemployment review (UB)	--	34	1	1	--
Liable relative work	2,035	2,331	53	58	9.4
Local office fraud work	1,437	1,697	24	27	12.5
Special investigation	496	612	32	40	25
Child benefit increase checks (cohabitation in relation to one-parent benefit)	--	60	1	1	--
	4,415	*5,640*	*£133m*	*£171m*	

An appendix to the statement dealt with the methods deployed to justify the alleged benefit savings. But first it was necessary to correct over-zealous claims—fraud officers, like fighter-pilots, are apparently liable to take an over-optimistic view of their successes. A revealing paragraph in the appendix stated that:

> Three separate, independent exercises were carried out between March and October 1980 aimed at establishing the accuracy of local office record-keeping. An element of over-recording was found and the following correction factors, based on these surveys, have been applied to savings claimed in 1980-81:

	Reduction %
Liable relative work	10
Local office fraud work	25
Special investigation	7½
Unemployment review	15

There was also a thorny problem of how long it should be assumed for the purpose of calculating savings that claimants who withdrew their claims or had their benefit stopped remained off benefit. The arbitrary figures chosen were multipliers of 17½ weeks for unemployment review cases, 52 weeks for fraud and special investigation, and none for liable relative work (because the amount can generally be precisely calculated from maintenance payments). It should be made clear that liable relative work is not necessarily anything to do with either fraud or abuse. It involves ensuring that payments are made by relatives liable in law to support claimants or members of their families (for instance, separated husbands and wives), and thereby can produce benefit savings. The liable relative may not resist his/her legal duty to provide this support. Similarly, unemployment review (that is, dealing with so-called 'voluntary unemployment') does not involve any necessary allegation of fraud or abuse; it is supposed to assist and encourage claimants back into work. Its function was described in 1973 as being 'to find why men are unable to obtain or to keep work and to help them, if practicable, to find a solution to any problem preventing them from doing so'.[11]

Once Patrick Jenkin had made his statement on savings, matters did not stand still. As the House of Commons was told: 'since 1981 DHSS have progressively reduced the additional complement of specialist staff, all of whom will be withdrawn by April 1983. To permit their final withdrawal DHSS are planning to reduce or abandon some of the anti-fraud activities which they consider to be least cost-effective.'[12]

Underneath all the razzamatazz, therefore, not everyone was convinced by this apparently successful campaign. Geoffrey Beltram was a high ranking civil servant in the DHSS at the time. Since retiring, he has written:

> The 1050 extra [fraud] staff would not have been made available, at a time of strict economy in civil service manpower, but for the expectation that their work would lead to substantial savings. However, for those not obliged to accept the political necessities which govern life in Whitehall, the question naturally arising was: what if some of the extra 1050 staff had been applied to encouraging take-up, or to improving the service generally?[13]

It seems possible that DHSS officials, while obliged to accept the 'political necessities' of staff cuts, used the excuse of fraud detection to delay the time when such cuts would fall heavily on the DHSS. Having done this, they then had to find the figures to justify their action. 'Creative accounting' appears to have been used to bolster up some decidedly shaky figures. The paradoxical, and often negative, effects of the DHSS resorting to such 'protectionist' tactics to defend staffing levels can also be seen in other areas of policy (see, for example, p 78).

Specialist Claims Control

Specialist Claims Control (SCC) teams were introduced into some regions in 1980, to tour local offices looking for certain types of fraud. Immediately, there was considerable criticism of the extensive powers the teams were given, and the fact that almost anyone could become the object of suspicion. The secretary of state grappled with these objections: 'Critics have argued that the arrangements under "specialist claims control" for stopping benefit are arbitrary and that oppressive tactics are used which in effect bully claimants into giving up their benefit. These criticisms are rejected, and stem from ignorance, or mischief, or both.' Nevertheless, two paragraphs later he revealed that: 'We are now developing fuller procedures for SCC, not because anything has gone wrong so far, but in recognition of its change from a regional initiative to a nationally applied method of fraud investigation.'[14] And in November 1981 SCC teams were introduced nationally, with a circular outlining their duties and the criteria for their work sent to all local offices.[15]

The fraud crusade was opposed by the two main civil service unions — the Society of Civil and Public Servants (SCPS) and the Civil and Public Servants Association (CPSA), who saw it as a diversion from the more important, if more routine, work in DHSS local offices (see Chapter 3). The charge brought specifically against SCC teams was that the techniques they employed involved essentially random investigation of claimants, using questionable interrogation techniques and unacceptable pressure to produce dubious savings, all in an atmosphere overcharged with the desire to meet targeted savings and root out fraud.[16]

Considerable effort was put into a team approach by SCC, who tried to create the esprit de corps of an elite. This approach spread to the Department of Employment (DE), where regional benefit investigation teams (RBITs or 'rabbits') were established in August 1983. Fraud investigators were linked up by local magazines. The flavour can be judged from excerpts from one such magazine published in the North of England.[17] A section entitled 'Prosecutions of Interest' affected a facetious style: 'Christmas came twice a year for a...claimant who was prosecuted last year for "working" as Santa Claus in a large department store. He was fined £50.' The magazine also claimed high patronage: 'Let there be no doubt that from the Prime Minister downwards there is concern about fraud and abuse of the benefit system and there is certainly no lessening of the priority of fraud work which ranks equally with other normal benefit work.' And, under 'The shape of things to come', it speculated on future trends:

> In general our policy has been to investigate only those cases of

fraud which have been brought to the Department's attention. We may call this a 'passive approach'. In future an active approach will be called for and techniques will be developed to uncover unsuspected fraudulent activity. Already some offices and the SIs [special investigators] have been involved to a limited degree in work of this kind. The message is that much more will be required in future, particularly from local fraud officers.

A report published in March 1981, from a team led by Sir Derek Rayner, alleged that 8 per cent of unemployed claimants were in fact working.[18] However, the report's foreword, by government ministers at the DE and the DHSS, cast doubt on the figure, and Sir Geoffrey Otton, permanent head of the DHSS, told the Public Accounts Committee that he also questioned it. The DHSS, he suggested, 'think that [it] may be too high. The trouble with this discussion is that it is all speculation in the absence of hard evidence.'[19] Nevertheless, down at the grass roots, amongst the anti-fraud workers themselves, the speculative figure was being used to boost activity: ' "Rayner" assumed 8%, so you can calculate the likely number on your own register if you accept that figure. Our detection rate is far short of that.'[20]

The most constant critics of SCC work have been the DHSS unions, the CPSA and the SCPS, even though most SCC members actually belong to the latter. The two unions jointly submitted five major objections to the operation of SCC in evidence to an internal review in 1982:[21]

• SCC teams disrupt usual office procedures and impede routine office administration.

• SCC teams choose their cases carefully—so that, for instance, they avoid those where the claimant is known to be violent or short-tempered; reject time-consuming cases; and 'take the easy cases of the fraud sections and leave the LO [local office] with the messy and time-consuming ones, thus making their own benefits savings look good at the expense of the LO'.

• SCC teams take on cases that are more appropriately handled elsewhere. In advance of an SCC visit, local offices hold back cases for special investigation so that SCC can have them.

• SCC visits cause a deterioration in relations between public and local office staff. 'SCC teams don't care if claimants are upset unnecessarily as they are only in the LO for a short while and don't have to pick up the pieces after they have gone.'

• SCC activity causes a variety of pressures to fall on staff, eg, 'Instances have come to light of HEOs [higher executive officers], with the apparent tacit approval of their supervisors, encouraging staff to overstep the mark with suggestions that you need to use bluff to achieve results; and when questioned, one HEO is quoted as saying "it is our job to achieve the targets set and justify the Government's figures".'

Sir Geoffrey Otton, appearing before the Public Accounts Committee, did not accept the existence of any such malpractices: 'There have been accusations that people are leaned on. But we have never had any evidence of this in more than a handful of cases and we have never had a substantiated case.'[22] Geoffrey Beltram gives a perhaps more balanced assessment: 'Common sense, and the fact that numbers of DHSS staff share the concern of claimants' representatives, also casts doubt on the view, implicit in one official statement, that *all* criticisms of SCC spring from ignorance, or mischief, or both.'[23]

Certainly, at one time in 1981, the route of one of the first SCC teams, as it progressed through the West Midlands, could be traced from the succession of complaining telephone calls to CPAG's Citizens Rights Office. Claimants so often described being locked into interviewing rooms that there must have been some substance to this complaint. Similarly, the allegation that SCC officers tore up benefit order books in front of claimants was repeated too often to be regarded as just hysterical or untrue. Claimants also consistently reported that they had undergone bullying and humiliating interviews.

Another allegation made in the West Midlands in 1981 was that SCC team members would promise single payments (lump-sum grants) to claimants if they would return to work. Two claimants complained to their local councillors when they got jobs but not the promised single payments. Such single payments were, in fact, not possible under the new benefit regulations introduced in November 1980. An internal inquiry established that locally produced training materials for investigators had not actually dealt with the changes to the benefit rules. The councillors obtained apologies and the claimants explanations. The cases got a certain amount of press coverage; but the decision of the inquiry was that bribery and inducement had not been substantiated.

Claimants frequently complained that their benefit had simply been stopped—seemingly in the hope that they would not reclaim. More precisely, the DHSS unions claimed that one SCC tactic was to stop batches of the forms ordering payments to unemployed claimants (B2/3s) from reaching the DE. It seems inconceivable that union members would invent such a specific allegation.

Local office union members particularly objected to the way in which the SCC calculated its benefit savings (as explained on pp 116-17). Union members reported an almost endless list of absurdities. For instance, a non-householder claimant receiving £16.35 per week was under suspicion of being 'voluntarily unemployed'; he went on a resettlement course, and so was paid £28.25

per week instead—yet benefit *savings* were claimed, of £16.35 x 52. One woman seen by an SCC officer turned out to be starting a job the very next day — the benefit saving was claimed nonetheless. Under examination by the Public Accounts Committee, Sir Geoffrey Otton said of the 52-week multiplier: 'There is obviously a difficult element of statistical calculation in all this and we are deploying some operational research people on it to see if we can achieve figures that are any different.'[24] To date, the operational research is not available.

Claimants' groups sprang into action in areas where SCC teams were due to operate and organised activities (sometimes with welfare rights organisations and with the unions) to impede the work of the teams, which relied heavily on self-incrimination. A revealing memorandum was prepared by an SCC team leader leaving Newcastle in January 1983:

> The success rate of the Team ... was below expectations. Factors which contributed to this was [sic] the adverse publicity instigated by Trade Unions and Welfare Rights organisations. This was aggravated to such an extent that leaflets were being distributed outside the office to all the claimants visiting there. That action was continued for about a fortnight. The leaflets did have some effect. When interviewing claimants it was noted that some hostility was engendered which prejudiced the normal success rate.

It has never been admitted that SCC tactics involved random investigation of claimants, although Geoffrey Beltram did make it clear that SCC teams 'carry out checks on individual claimants, drawn chiefly from among the unemployed and single parents, and selected because they have certain characteristics commonly found in cases of fraud... Generally, the cases selected present no specific indications of fraud.'[25]

Norwich Citizens Advice Bureau (CAB) had a similar experience when a DE 'rabbit' team visited the city between mid-October and Christmas 1983. The CAB workers discussed various complaints with the team leader, who explained his understanding of the current position to them:

> the setting up of the original Benefit Investigation Teams was a result of a change of emphasis in fraud investigation. In the past the Department had relied on information received from other members of the public, other claimants etc. It was now the intention of the Department to use these Investigation Teams to interview at random in the hope of uncovering fraudulent claims. He agreed that it was possible therefore that legitimate claimants could be interviewed in this way.[26]

The department referred to here is the DE, but there is no reason to think that the DHSS had a different perception, at least when SCC was set up. Sir Geoffrey Otton talked to the Public Accounts Committee in March 1983 of 'grasping the nettle' of random investigation as a future possibility.[27]

Finally, however, in June 1983 the DHSS, tacitly admitting that some of these criticisms were justified, produced a new draft of the circular (FIG/21) outlining the role of SCC teams. The differences between the first and second drafts demonstrate clearly that the criteria to be used in selecting cases for investigation had been dramatically narrowed. The changes covered both the classes of claimants to be targeted by SCC and the methods to be used. The first circular had authorised random checks of any unemployed claimant who was not ill. The second sought to remove the random element. The two wide-ranging 'targeting' criteria omitted in the second circular were:

> (f) the claimant is apparently fit and in good health (ie, is not in receipt of the incapacity/disablement benefits and no report by a Visiting Officer contains a reference to the claimant's poor health)...
> (g) (unless there is some clear indication of fraud) current unemployment has lasted for more than four months...

Another criterion was significantly amended by the addition of the words emphasised here: 'the claimant has a record of self-employment *of a sort which suggests that, even in the current economic situation, he might be able to engage in some profitable activity*.' The criteria which remained unchanged were: where there was a report of possible fraud already; where an unemployment review officer requested SCC intervention; and where the claimant had previously worked in the kind of job that could be done on a casual or part-time basis. A new criterion was added to the later circular, covering those with relatives known to be in business or self-employment.

The language of the second circular also changed significantly. The somewhat sneering tone of the earlier draft had gone. For example, the initial criteria for investigating claimants included cases in which 'the claimant has a skill—eg, typing, car repairs... and local knowledge indicates opportunities for him to work "on the side".' This became 'local knowledge indicates *that there are local job opportunities for him*'. The later circular also asked SCC officers to tell claimants if they had been exonerated: 'A word of explanation and reassurance will help to counter the adverse publicity which SCC has attracted.'

Much the same process of 'toning down' took place in the section on the criteria for selecting 'liable relatives' cases for investigation. There were significant changes, too, in advice on interviewing techniques. Claimants had consistently complained that they were ostentatiously locked into interviewing rooms by SCC officers. This was always denied; nonetheless, the wording of one section in the first circular which had read: 'a person who has something to hide is likely to feel uncomfortable if he has been specifically called in to a Government Office for an interview', became instead: 'If the interview takes place at the LO [local office] care should be taken to avoid giving the impression that the interview room has been locked to prevent the claimant from leaving.' Also out from the list of 'acceptable techniques' of interviewing went the 'hard' and 'soft' interrogation, as spelt out in the earlier circular: '[if two officers are involved in the interview] leave one to concentrate on understanding the claimant's circumstances and problems while the other concentrates on safeguarding public funds.'

It is commendable that the DHSS should have responded so positively. Whether, in fact, the new guidance has altogether changed SCC methods of operation on the ground is another question. As recently as the summer of 1984, the DHSS unions produced a leaflet to be given to claimants, advocating (in duly balanced language) non-cooperation with SCC teams.[28]

Operation Major

When Reg Prentice announced the anti-fraud drive in 1980, he implied that the campaign would include a strong emphasis on using publicity. In practice, the DHSS has been more equivocal:

> There are arguments for and against a SCC Team's activities. On the one hand, knowledge that the Department is making a special effort in an area may prompt some claimants to withdraw unjustified claims. On the other hand, publicity about SCC exercises has had undesirable consequences in some areas.[29]

Whatever the 'official' line, publicity was certainly used to sensational effect in the handling of 'Operation Major'.

On 2 September 1982 the DHSS held a joint press conference with the Thames Valley police that was designed to produce maximum coverage for its anti-fraud drive. Operation Major, which resulted in the arrest of large numbers of claimants, accused of fraudulently claiming benefits from an address at which they were not in fact residents, was made *very* public.[30] The press coverage, which linked the operation with the DHSS's general fraud work and, more specifically, with SCC,[31] was enormous. Some of the content of the presentation by the DHSS and the police at the press conference can be gathered from the fact that three different newspapers used the plot of the film 'The Sting' as an analogy.

There was also a striking measure of agreement about the figure of £1.5m as the likely benefit savings from the raid. The *Sun*, *Daily Star*, *Daily Mail*, *Daily Express*, *The Times* and ITN all quoted this figure. Both the police and the DHSS deny mentioning it; and Sir Geoffrey Otton was adamant about this to the Public Accounts Committee: 'We are not responsible for that figure and never were. We did not set out on Operation Major in order to achieve any particular level of benefit savings.'[32] However, no one accused the journalists of inventing the figure.

As time went on, it became clear that the prospective benefit savings were nowhere near £1.5m; that one-third of the 286 people arrested were completely innocent; and that the DHSS and the police between them had failed to obtain any evidence against the landlord, who, both alleged, had been the ultimate target. More disturbingly, it was revealed that the DHSS knew exactly how many people were registered as staying in the building. Aware of its maximum capacity of 90, the DHSS had watched while the numbers rose well above that. Figures were given out for the number of claimants registered at the address for various dates in 1982: by 5 May the number had gone above the 90 mark, by 15 July it had reached 185 and by 25 August, 255 (and on 2 September, 290 were registered).[33] The DHSS local office manager, John Minchell, told a court that visits ceased to the property in early June 1982. As CHAR commented:

> The police figures, Rossi's House of Commons' statement [that the DHSS spotted a sudden rise of claimants in early July] and Minchell's evidence in court about DHSS visits point strongly to a deliberate policy of stepping back from the scene and allowing numbers to rise in order to 'catch' a maximum number of claimants.[34]

Yet, when questioned about Operation Major, Sir Geoffrey Otton told the Public Accounts Committee that 'this kind of itinerant fraud is not in fact one of the most serious areas of fraud for us, simply because of the limited number of people involved nationally'.[35] This makes it even more difficult not to believe that the operation, with its built-in bid for massive publicity, was planned as a deterrent, not only against this specific and 'limited' type of fraud, but against fraud generally; and that the DHSS consciously colluded with those defrauding it in the months running up to the operation in order to maximise its public impact. The end result was a deliberately manufactured demonstration of 'strong-arm' tactics against a vulnerable group of claimants (see Chapter 6). It seems unlikely that its longer-term effects will include Reg Prentice's declared aim of creating 'a better atmosphere in which people will not be inhibited from claiming their benefit'.[36]

Conclusion

The danger for the future is clear. The pressures on DHSS staffing may become so acute that the anti-fraud techniques described in this chapter may develop into a completely random sampling of claimants. This would mean that, instead of the proper and due administration of claims, control would be maintained on the basis of the claimant's fear that he or she would be selected for examination. In organisational terms, it would mean a further switch from home visiting by staff from local offices to touring regional investigative teams. This shift is already proving damaging, and should be reversed rather than developed further, for several crucial reasons:

• The tradition of home visiting — though sometimes seen as hostile by claimants — does involve considering whether a claimant qualifies for any *extra* benefit as much as whether any payment can be reduced. Recent monitoring reports, for instance that by Berthoud,[37] have demonstrated how crucial home visits can be, especially in ensuring that claimants receive single payments.

• The diversion of staff into fraud work has undermined the DHSS's ability to cope with routine administration and to ensure that every claimant gets his/her full entitlement to benefit — let alone to begin to reach out to the one in four people entitled to SB who do not claim it. The diversion of 1,050 experienced staff into fraud work immediately prior to November 1980 cannot have improved the DHSS's capacity to cope with the massive changes to the SB scheme introduced in the same month. Whilst the rising proportion of claimants to staff is one of the major causes of the crisis in administration in the DHSS, more resources would have been available to deal with this had they not been hived off to concentrate on anti-fraud work.

• Random investigation intrudes on a claimant's civil liberties. It is fundamentally at odds with the right of the citizen to be treated as innocent until proved guilty. Fraud investigation is not only about the recovery of overpayment; it involves allegations of the commission of a criminal offence. There should be no sphere of life in which the citizen can be called in and subjected to interview to prove that he or she has *not* committed an offence.

• The whole notion of the savings to be obtained from fraud work is suspect. The 'success' of initiatives since 1979 looks questionable if the methods of calculating benefit savings are analysed in any depth.

• The emphasis on fraud does have effects on honest claimants and prospective claimants. The recent anti-fraud emphasis in the DHSS must bear some responsibility for the deepening crisis of confidence in the benefits system as a whole. As Geoffrey Beltram has written:

> From talking with claimants and people in touch with claimants, the conclusion is inescapable that in some cases the general climate of suspicion in the country has aggravated loss of self-esteem and dislike of claiming SB, with some negative if unmeasurable effect on take-up.[38]

Of Reg Prentice's two opinions, quoted on page 114, one can only say that he was right first time.

References

1 DHSS press release, 11 January 1979.
2 *House of Commons Hansard*, 9 March 1971, cols 252-3.
3 As note 1 above.
4 *Tribune*, 22 February 1980.
5 DHSS press release, 13 February 1980.
6 Comptroller and Auditor General, *2nd Report of the Committee of Public Accounts*, 7 November 1983, para 21, HC102.
7 G Beltram, *Testing the Safety Net*, Bedford Square Press 1984, p 107.
8 Amendment to *Fraud Investigators' Guide*, Serial No 4, June 1980.
9 DHSS press release, 6 May 1981.
10 As note 9.
11 *Report of the Committee on Abuse of Social Security Benefits*, HMSO 1973, p 113.
12 Memorandum by the Comptroller and Auditor General, *2nd Report of the Public Accounts Committee 1983-84*, para 11, HC102.
13 As note 7, p 101.
14 *House of Commons Hansard*, 6 May 1981, cols 79-80.
15 *House of Commons Hansard*, 28 February 1984, col 227.
16 eg, *Note of a National Conference on DHSS Fraud (Specialist Claims Control), Saturday 24th September 1983* (SCPS and CPSA) 1983.
17 *Fraud Information Bulletin*, Department of Employment, Leeds.
18 *Payment of Benefits to Unemployed People*, Department of Employment/DHSS, March 1981.
19 See note 6 above, para 1779.
20 See note 17 above.
21 Evidence submitted to the DHSS Operational Research Services Study into SCC, June 1982.
22 See note 6 above, para 1735.
23 See note 7 above, p 102.
24 See note 6 above, para 1698.
25 See note 7 above, p 101.
26 *Report* by Organiser, Regional Benefit Investigation Team, 5 January 1984.
27 See note 6 above, para 1779.
28 SCPS/CPSA, 'Claiming benefit'.
29 FIG/21, para 9.
30 Operation Major is covered in depth in Ros Franey, *Poor Law: the mass arrest of homeless claimants in Oxford*, CPAG, CHAR, Claimants Defence Committee, NAPO and NCCL 1983, and *Fraud and Operation Major: an assessment*, CHAR 1983.
31 See, for instance, *The Times*, 4 September 1982, *Sun*, 3 September 1982,

and *Standard*, 6 September 1982, and analysed in *Poor Law* (see note 30 above).

32 See note 6 above, para 1763.

33 See *Fraud and Operation Major*, note 30 above, p 9.

34 As note 33 above.

35 See note 6 above, para 1762.

36 See note 5 above.

37 R Berthoud, *The Reform of Supplementary Benefit*, Policy Studies Institute 1984.

38 See note 7 above, p 93.

10. Conclusion: closed doors and closing options

FRAN BENNETT

'No document within living memory has made such a powerful impression, or stirred such hopes, as the Beveridge Report.'[1]

This book began with an assessment of the 'hidden agenda' of the government's social security reviews (see Chapter 1). The 'government paper of some colour'[2] conveying the government's plans for the future of social security provision should be ready shortly after this book's publication. At this stage, the specific proposals resulting from the reviews must be a matter for conjecture. It is doubtful, though, whether any proposals for change will be given the same near-unanimous welcome as the Beveridge Report — despite Norman Fowler's frequent (and, no doubt, sincere) protestations that the reviews should be seen as an exercise of similar scope.[3] It is much more likely that the government, having started by asking the wrong questions, will come up with the wrong answers.

In this conclusion, CPAG's perspective on the reviews is outlined: our initial doubts about their form and function — which have been confirmed, rather than dispelled, by subsequent developments; the major points put forward in our written and oral evidence; and our definition of the right starting-point for a comprehensive review of the purposes, present structure and future direction of income maintenance and distribution.

Reviews under wraps

Given the three agendas for the reviews, identified by Sue Ward in Chapter 1,[4] it was inevitable that official sources would be very unclear about the exact aims and contents of the various examinations being conducted by the review teams. It was overwhelmingly evident from the outset, however, that these were to be 'reviews under wraps'. None of the written and oral evidence submitted to the reviews was to be published. As the then Minister for Social Security wrote in response to an early letter from CPAG urging publication, 'people putting evidence are perfectly free to publish it themselves'.[5] More seriously, it appeared that the reports of the individual review teams were not to be published either, but would be submitted direct to Norman Fowler, Secretary of State for Social Services. A 'central co-ordinating unit' of civil servants within the DHSS, to which neither individual members of the public nor interested groups had open access, was to undertake the unenviable task of attempting to mesh the proposals of the different teams into a coherent whole. The final—indeed, the only—formal publication to emerge from the whole process will be the government's 'Green Paper or other public document'.[6]

CPAG, along with other organisations across the political spectrum, argued from the start that, regardless of whether a 'secret agenda' existed, the government should at least not keep the 'minutes' secret in this way. There was broad concern, too, about the whistle-stop speed of the reviews themselves. Nicholas Timmins of *The Times* described the reviews as having 'an ambitiously tight timetable';[7] and in another article pointed out that 'if Mr Fowler really wants the open debate he claims, he should match his actions to his words. The Newton and Boyson reports should be published. The succeeding paper should be green and not white'.[8] From some quarters, of course, the call for a wider and more public debate was prompted by another motive—the fear that secrecy would guarantee any 'radical' (ie, cost-cutting) government proposals the same hostile reception that greeted the leaked Think Tank report on welfare state spending in 1982, forcing the government to label it a 'dead duck'.[9] Claimants' organisations and left-wing groups, on the other hand, saw the reviews unambiguously as a put-up job, with so-called independent members—in reality, government puppets—placed there to endorse proposals formulated well before the public relations exercise of the reviews was launched.[10]

In private letters to the chairs of three of the review teams, in an open letter to the secretary of state (published jointly with other organisations) and in a further joint letter to *The Times*,[11] CPAG argued that the promise of 'open discussion' when the reviews were announced[12] would only be credible if the government itself facilitated a wide public debate. Ironically, the rushed timetable imposed by the government for the submission of written evidence, and the coincidence of the deadline of 31 July with the beginning of the so-called 'silly season' for the media (when there was little other news), together ensured that a lively debate on the reviews did, in fact, take place throughout the summer. The 'quality press', at least, reported on the major submissions as they appeared at regular intervals,[13] and editorials and letters often followed.

1984: changed priorities ahead?—CPAG's evidence

Several groups decided to draw up one document which they then sent as evidence to all the review teams. CPAG instead concentrated on the specific questions raised in the individual consultation documents, and sent in separate submissions to the reviews of benefits for children and young people, supplementary benefit (SB) and housing benefit (HB). It did, however, address more general issues in an Appendix, a copy of which was sent to each review team with the written evidence. A shortened version of the Appendix is reprinted on pp 144-47.[14]

Benefits for children and young people

Announcing the reviews in the House of Commons, Norman Fowler described one of their central aims as being: 'to channel [the available resources] to where they are most needed'.[15] This phrase has traditionally been used as a euphemism for means-testing. Given that two of the reviews were dealing with benefits which are already means-tested (HB and SB), it seemed probable from the outset that the Department of Health and Social Security (DHSS) intended the review of benefits for children and young people to be the vehicle for the scrutiny of possible further extensions of means-testing. In addition, if the Treasury was pressing for cuts in public expenditure in order to finance tax cuts, the only benefit besides pensions which could yield the appropriate level of 'savings' was child benefit.

In this context, CPAG's evidence to this review[16] had to be fairly defensive in tone and content. We therefore repeated familiar arguments about the important functions of child benefit — to prevent poverty among families with children; to ease the poverty and unemployment traps in a cost-effective way; to give women access to a source of independent income; and to achieve equity within the taxation system between those with and those without children. We devoted considerable space to an explanation of the principled and pragmatic arguments against the restriction of child benefit through either means-testing or (under the current tax system) making it subject to taxation. We set out the first vital steps on the road to a simplified, rational and equitable system of child support: a gradual increase in the level of child benefit until it subsumed the child support paid to long-term national insurance beneficiaries, and therefore provided the same level of benefit to children regardless of whether their parents were in or out of employment. We also asked for consideration to be given to making child benefit age-related, to reflect the higher costs of older children; and to a special addition, paid to all families with a child under school age, to take account of their vulnerability to poverty caused by the restriction of women's employment opportunities at that stage of the lifecycle.

The government's restriction of options for change to those which can be contained 'within the present overall level of social security expenditure'[17] in theory rules out the adoption of any of these proposals. This imposition of an arbitrary financial ceiling is an absurd and artificial limitation of debate, as the case of child benefit shows. Child benefit was only brought completely within the social security budget within the last decade, when it replaced family allowances and child tax allowances. Tax reliefs and allowances have the same effect on the government's finances as cash benefits: the government either has to raise money in taxation or to borrow it to cover the cost of both. However, although tax reliefs and allowances cost about the same in total as the social security budget, they do not count as public spending in the government's accounts, and there are no annual debates over whether they should be cut back to reduce the total of public expenditure. If child tax allowances still existed today, therefore, they would not be subject to the nil-cost restraint imposed on the social security reviews. As CPAG pointed out in its evidence, it is high time to end these public accounting conventions, which succeed only in distorting debate and decisions about income maintenance and distribution.

There is also a growing and broad range of opinion which favours phasing out the anachronistic married man's tax allowance for those below pension age, and using most of the resources thus released to increase child benefit substantially.[18] The terms of reference of the reviews seem to preclude the consideration of any such proposal, since it would nominally 'increase' the social security budget by over £3½ billion in this tax year alone. The fact that it would simultaneously raise the government's receipts from tax revenue by the same amount, and so would merely represent a transfer of resources between groups of people, would be ignored. That such a one-eyed view of 'public spending' should dictate the shape of provision for children in the future seems nothing short of farcical.

Janet Allbeson demonstrated in Chapter 7 (pp 81-99) that young people in the 16 to 20 age range have been an easy target for benefit cuts over the last few years. Early in the review process, Dr Rhodes Boyson himself rightly identified current financial provision for teenagers as a 'tangle'.[19] With a few notable exceptions, such as Youthaid and the National Union of Students, there is a lack of identifiable pressure groups enlisted in their cause. This not only makes young people a vulnerable group policitally (see Chapter 7), but also contributes to a paucity of policies to solve the present 'tangle' of benefits.

There is certainly a serious and so far unresolved problem, but the trend of recent government policies affecting young people does not hold out the promise of a satisfactory solution. The injunction in the consultation document to those giving evidence to consider the 'stability of families' in any proposals for change may indicate further threats to push teenagers back into the bosom of their families, by taking away their right to claim SB as individuals when unemployed.

CPAG argued in its evidence that such moves would be unacceptable, even as a 'quid pro quo' for improvements in financial provision for other young people. The most likely improvement would be some form of national scheme of educational maintenance allowances (EMAs). CPAG recently put forward proposals for a non-means-tested statutory system of EMAs, paid at the level of the Youth Training Scheme (YTS) allowance to young people themselves.[20] We repeated this suggestion in our evidence to the review team, pointing out that the lack of any coherent provision for teenagers at school aged 16 or over was the most glaring anomaly in the treatment of young people at present. There is no 'cost-free' solution, however, which would not involve trade-offs harming other young people who could ill afford to lose out. The finances to ensure that all young people have a real choice at the minimum school-leaving age should be regarded in the same way as the resources provided for the recent introduction of YTS: an investment in the country's future. Unfortunately, the provision of adequate EMAs does not have the same political appeal—especially only two years into the government's second term of office—as did the creation of a new training scheme in the run-up to the general election of 1983. Political considerations may once again prejudice the achievement of a more rational system of financial provision for young people as a result of the review team's investigations.

Housing benefit

As Nick Raynsford's account shows (see Chapter 5), the introduction of the new HB scheme in 1982/3 will go down in the annals of social policy development as an administrative disaster. Very few amongst those responsible for its invention and implementation would now claim otherwise. One DHSS minister, who did not wish to be identified, has described it as 'the biggest labyrinth since classical times'. The scheme has been constantly revised since its introduction, and this has added to the administrative chaos.

In its evidence,[21] CPAG concentrated on refuting the government's claim that HB was going too far up the income scale—and on pointing out the double standards which allow the government, on the one hand, to penalise HB claimants by deploying such arguments, whilst, on the other, increasing the ceiling for mortgage interest tax relief (and continuing to give proportionately more relief to those rich enough to pay the higher rates of income tax). The consultation document for the HB review specifically instructed those giving evidence that 'the review . . . is not concerned . . . with income tax relief on mortgage interest'.[22]

The HB review team, unlike the other review teams, was entirely independent of the government. CPAG, therefore, in common with other groups, urged its members to express their concern to the government that this deliberate exclusion of mortgage interest tax relief from the terms of reference precluded any sensible discussion of whether the HB scheme was in fact over-generous—let alone any consideration of proposals for the rational reform of housing finance and subsidy arrangements as a whole. We did, however, put forward short-term proposals for the transfer of the responsibility for HB from local authorities to the DHSS, and for the exploration of a truly 'unified' HB scheme for all those on low incomes.

Unfortunately, the independence of the HB review team appears to owe much more to the government's desire to distance itself from the unmitigated disaster of the present scheme than to any readiness to accept criticism or proposals for change from an external body. The impression CPAG and other voluntary organisations have gained is that its members are unlikely to take up the invitation to point out the limitations imposed by their terms of reference. The arrangements for oral evidence sessions made by this team were even less open and flexible than those made by the teams involving government ministers. Hearings were not open to the public, dates offered were not allowed to be varied, and there was a maximum of two participants per organisation.

It seems unlikely that the review team will challenge the government's attempt to narrow the debate on HB to a consideration of how to simplify administration and further restrict its scope. Another opportunity to initiate a debate on housing finance and subsidies as a whole will have been missed.

Supplementary benefit

The consultation document for the SB review is a masterpiece in the art of deliberately missing the point—so much so that, at times, it takes on a tragicomic tone. The introduction to the document defines one of the main problems in the current scheme as 'the complexity of the rules which relate support closely to individual circumstances, combined with the mass role the scheme continues to play', and declares that 'no other country operates such a centralised and detailed system to supplement basic income support'. It goes on to list one of the key issues for consultation as 'whether there are alternative ways of providing means-tested help for several million people'.[23]

There is no mention of the fact that most other major industrialised countries with which the UK should compare itself have a system of more generous (often earnings-related) *non*-means-tested benefits for various qualifying groups; or that many have higher family benefits and a national minimum wage in addition. The authors do not seem to recognise that the suggestion they put forward, of 'schemes providing benefits for broad groups of claimants with less emphasis on individual circumstances', would be an attempt to recreate within a means-tested framework the structure appropriate to a non-means-tested benefits system such as the national insurance scheme. In the document's potted history of the SB scheme over the last few years, there is no acknowledgment that one of the reasons for the growing numbers of SB claimants — and hence the growing pressure on staff and claimants alike — has been the government's cuts in those non-means-tested benefits.

CPAG said in its evidence to the SB review:

> The SB scheme is inherently costly and complex to administer . . . Supplementary benefit is being forced to play a role for which it was never designed and never intended. The numbers on SB continue to rise because of the failure of the rest of the social security system.[24]

Just as in the last review of the SB scheme, however,[25] the government appears once again to be trying to find an administrative solution within the SB scheme itself to problems whose nature is not administrative and whose origins lie largely outside the scheme itself. The 'key issues for consultation'[26] do not include a major problem identified by the recent research into the post-1980 SB scheme:[27] the inadequacy of current benefit levels, in particular for families with children and the long-term unemployed, who are thereby excluded from participation in the life of the community. CPAG has argued consistently that benefit rates for children should be raised as a matter of urgency, and that the long-term unemployed should be given access to the higher long-term rate of SB on the same terms as other long-term claimants.[28] We repeated these demands as our most urgent priorities in our evidence.

The consultation documents identified 'simplification' of the benefits system as one of the central aims of the reviews, and Norman Fowler emphasised the particular complexity of SB in his announcement of the reviews in the House of Commons.[29] CPAG warned in its evidence that the most obvious route to simplification — the abolition of many of the additional weekly payments and lump-sum grants to SB claimants — would be unacceptable, unless it was carried out on the principle of no losses to the beneficiaries. This means that slightly higher benefit rates for selected groups of 'deserving' claimants would not be a sufficient quid pro quo for major cutbacks in special payments. The sort of 'trade-off' made in the last SB review, which resulted in slightly higher weekly benefit rates for some children, but a severe cutback in the availability of single payments for clothing and footwear to families,[30] must not be repeated. Simplification for administrators means increased hardship for the most needy claimants, unless more money is available for improvements in the scheme. The administrative crisis within the DHSS must not be solved at claimants' expense.

In any case, these additional payments are only 'one small area of complexity in a scheme which has many, many more'.[31] The equal treatment regulations, for example, are so complicated that the vast majority of DHSS staff and claimants probably do not understand them. A means-tested scheme of the magnitude of SB is, in fact, inherently complex, and many of its more complicated procedures are to do with the testing of resources (both income and capital), rather than with the payment of benefits.

The central statements in our evidence to the review team, underpinning our more detailed proposals, were twofold. First, that the acceptance of the 'mass role' of SB in the last SB review was a major step in the wrong direction: 'the true role of SB remains as a residual scheme, underpinning a comprehensive system of adequate, non-means-tested, non-contributory benefits'.[32] Implicit in this definition of SB was our belief—shared by many others giving evidence to the review—that it is futile to consider SB in isolation from other elements of the social security system.

Secondly, we pointed to the 'considerable body of evidence' indicating that present SB levels are too low, and urged the government to commission research which, for the first time since the 1930s, would attempt to set a 'poverty line' adequate to allow SB claimants to 'participate in the life of the community'.[33] Again, a large number of other organisations giving evidence to the review echoed this call.[34]

Reviews under way

A common concern about the reviews was their apparently fragmented and partial nature. In CPAG's journal, we described them as a 'hotch-potch of overlapping inquiries, some looking at specific groups of claimants and others at specific benefits'.[35] They did not appear to add up to a coherent examination of the social security system as a whole, let alone the other major determinants of income distribution such as the taxation and wages systems.

Many other organisations criticised the piecemeal nature of the reviews, some calling instead for a Royal Commission to be set up to undertake an appropriately long-term and coherent examination of all the issues at stake.[36]

As the reviews proceeded, however, there were indications that wider issues *were* under consideration, and that the central principles of the welfare state were being re-examined with a view to possible changes of a fundamental nature. Some press reports immediately after Norman Fowler's announcement suggested that a major shake-up of the social security system was being set in motion.[37] However, it only gradually became evident that such reports, whilst they might not be correct in every detail, had at least accurately identified the nature and extent of the re-think which the reviews represented.

It emerged, for example, that the 'central coordinating unit' of civil servants within the DHSS was not only coordinating the results of the various reviews, but also examining some of the areas of overlap (such as the poverty and unemployment traps). The Conservative Research Department itself informed us that the unit was 'identifying wider issues — those crossing the boundaries of more than one review — and seeing that they are carefully examined'; and that its job was also to 'monitor...the progress of the reviews for the Secretary of State, so that he can ensure that there is a consistent and coherent approach between them'.[38]

These phrases begin to sound remarkably like the comprehensive overview whose absence many people, including CPAG, were deploring. The snag, of course, was that such questions were to be asked, and answered, by a small team of civil servants, rather than by a process of open debate and public discussion. Other government departments could presumably take the opportunity of making their views known to the unit. One policy option, for example, known to be dear to the Treasury's heart — the integration of income tax and national insurance contributions — was mentioned in the press as an idea to be considered during the reviews.[39] No denial was issued by the DHSS; yet it was difficult to see how this option could be considered under any of the headings of the reviews themselves. It was never made clear officially whether the central coordinating unit would, amongst its other tasks, be chatting to the Treasury about issues such as this — although an article in the *Financial Times* suggested that the Treasury did have direct access to the review teams.[40] A letter to *The Times* from CPAG and other organisations, calling on the government to 'give a clear and definitive list of the issues under consideration',[41] was ignored.

The oral hearings were the setting for further demonstrations of the elastic nature of the reviews' agendas. Groups giving oral evidence were faced with questions of a much broader nature than those addressed in the consultation documents — such as their opinion of the contributory national insurance system or of proposals for negative income tax schemes. This sudden leap from the particular to the general was most evident in the review of benefits for children and young people, which, it appeared, was being used as the forum for discussion of the purpose and scope of social security provision in general. Thus, almost every participant was asked his/her view of the role of the welfare state: is it to relieve poverty? is it to redistribute income? and so on.[42]

It is hard to see the value of any conclusion drawn from the various off-the-cuff answers to this crucial question, directed at individuals who had not been warned in advance that this was one of a standard half-dozen questions. However, it was increasingly evident from the reactions of the review team members that the 'correct' answer, so far as they were concerned, was that the overriding aim of the welfare state must be the relief of poverty. Had participants been aware from the start that this review was examining such wide-ranging questions, they might have been better prepared. As it was, many groups giving the 'correct' answer may find that they have unwittingly lent their support to government moves towards greater selectivity in the social security system, via an extention of means-testing. For, while 'the relief of poverty' may at first sight seem a laudable goal, it demonstrates a distressingly narrow view of the various functions of social security provision (see Chapter 1, pp 4-5). If such an aim were to be seen as the only justification for spending on social security benefits, it would mean not only abandoning the wider redistributive role of income support, but also openly declaring that the *prevention* of poverty had been struck from the list of desirable social objectives.

Conclusion

Thus, there is a growing volume of evidence to suggest that what, at first sight, appeared to be another attempt to 'tinker' with bits and pieces of the social security system is providing the backdrop for some fundamental rethinking by ministers and civil servants of the objectives and structure of the social security system. Indeed, Tony Newton told the Conservative Party Conference in the autumn that 'we are in the business not of tinkering but of reform'.[43]

To some extent, the government was already being pushed in the direction of radical change by several groups submitting evidence to the reviews. In addition to the right-wing organisations mentioned by Sue Ward (see p 12), three different packages have been put forward by the National Consumer Council (NCC), the National Council for Voluntary Organisations (NCVO), and members of the Institute for Fiscal Studies (IFS).[44] All three had, in fact, been developing their blueprints for some time before the reviews were even announced, but took this opportunity to display them to public view.

The three groups have another factor in common, too. None of them is best known for familiarity with, or expert knowledge of, the benefits system. The NCC has an interest in all issues affecting consumers; the NCVO acts as a coordinating body for voluntary organisations; and the IFS has, deservedly, acquired a reputation for its expertise in relation to the taxation system. The 'outsiders' view' shared by the three gives them a refreshing originality: dilemmas familiar to workers in the social security field are discussed from a radically different standpoint, or dismissed as unimportant or out-of-date in a changed and changing world. They find a route through the wood, rather than stopping to examine every tree. There are problems and dangers, however, in attempting to present the government with a blueprint for change, especially when (as with the IFS and NCVO schemes, in particular) the solution proposed involves a radical departure from current principles and practice. As Professor Tony Atkinson has pointed out on several occasions, it is often suspiciously easy to demonstrate that a hypothetical scheme will work much more smoothly than the present system, whose faults in practice are only too apparent.[45]

The overriding concentration on one or two principles, and the mechanisms necessary to put them into practice, can blind the proponents of particular schemes to crucial issues. The IFS has taken to heart some (though not all) of the objections to means-testing, for example, which have been voiced by the 'poverty lobby' over the years: that it is a divisive, stigmatising and humiliating mechanism for income distribution to the poor. It therefore attempts, through applying a means test (in theory, at least) to the whole population, and by routing it through an 'automated' tax/benefit system, to remove such objections — although, as Jonathan Bradshaw has made clear in Chapter 8, it has by no means succeeded.

The NCVO is also conscious of the arguments against means-testing, and against other conditions of qualification for benefit such as 'signing on' as available for work; its solution is to propose that everyone, both in and out of employment, should be given a basic benefit as of right, with no conditions attached. Neither the IFS nor the NCVO seems to think that the level of benefit awarded might be a crucial consideration from the claimant's perspective; indeed, both groups see it as a positive virtue of their proposed schemes that they would be flexible to adoption and adaptation by governments with widely varying political perspectives —

including, presumably, radically different ideas about the appropriate level of benefit for the poor.[46]

When criticised for this apparent blind spot, both groups could argue that the present social security scheme has proved its vulnerability to attack under governments of differing political persuasions. The IFS and the NCVO are both convinced that the present structure of benefit provision is beyond repair and must be abandoned entirely. Many of their criticisms are cogent and justified. What is rather disturbing about their at times virulent critique is the way in which it uses the social security system as a scapegoat for problems external to it.[47] *Any* benefits system subjected to the twin forces of mass unemployment and a government intent on devoting more resources to the better-off will be put under extreme pressure.[48] It is far from clear whether either the IFS or the NCVO model schemes would, in fact, perform any better than the existing system when caught in a similar pincer movement.

As one commentator in the *Financial Times* wrote recently, 'the existing, flawed system [may be] a reasonable, if unintended, compromise between three different approaches to social security'.[49] Each of the three organisations proposes, in essence, the extension of one element of the existing social security scheme at the expense of others. The IFS wants almost all benefits to be income-related, and repeats the superficially attractive arguments for selectivity and means-tested provision. The NCVO supports universal benefits, with no tests of either income or contribution record. The NCC puts forward a revitalised contributory scheme, though with greatly relaxed contribution conditions and greatly reduced means-tested supplementation. Given the attempts, by at least one review team, to narrow the purpose of social security provision to 'the relief of poverty' alone, it is likely that the IFS scheme is the model under the closest scrutiny by the government at the moment.

Whilst 'there are quite strong arguments for and against each' of these approaches[50] — especially if advanced in their most 'pure' form — all three at least represent studies of the social security system in its entirety, which deliberately and openly focus on questions of purpose and principle. The fact that they come to radically different conclusions as a result of their enquiries demonstrates that there *is* a wide range of opinions about the desirable direction for the future of social security provision in this country.

By contrast, the government's reviews have shown a desperate desire to close off some options for change, and to discuss others only behind closed doors. Many possibilities were immediately ruled out of court by the imposition of a nil-cost remit; no matter how good a case might be made for improvements, they would not be made if they cost more money.

Fundamental questions, such as the role of the welfare state, were not introduced into the review process until quite late in the whole process—at the stage of oral hearings—and only one answer appeared to be acceptable. Other broader issues are being considered, not in open session, but by the 'central coordinating unit' in secret. Recent press reports have suggested that the final discussions of proposals for change have been blanketed in an atmosphere of official secrecy usually reserved for national security issues.[51] The written and oral evidence to the reviews is not being published. The government's conclusions are. But they are likely to take the form of a White Paper—or a Green Paper with white edges—with little opportunity to change any of the proposals it contains.

The reviews need not have been conducted in this manner. Indeed, the government had a model for its 'great debate'[52] already on the shelves, in the form of a draft report from the House of Commons Treasury and Civil Service Committee published in 1983.[53] This report was the end product of a comprehensive examination of the interaction of the taxation and social security system, by a special sub-committee, chaired by Michael Meacher MP. It contained a range of both short-term and longer-term alternatives for steps towards a more rational and equitable system of income distribution. The government seems to have chosen to ignore the findings of this report, despite its thorough appraisal of the problems, and its coherent proposals for change in both the social security and taxation systems. This is a pity. Although the sub-committee's study, which formed the basis of the committee's draft report, excluded a detailed appraisal of benefits for those not in employment, its method of working provided a model for any similar study. It received written evidence from numerous sources, heard oral evidence in public sessions, and involved MPs on an all-party basis. The whole process took place over more than a year. The written and oral evidence was published, and research was commissioned on specific questions. The sub-committee refused to be bound by arbitrary definitions of public spending, and so included the 'hidden welfare state' of tax reliefs and allowances in its deliberations; and it was not afraid to ignore artificial departmental boundaries in its conclusions.

CPAG believes that there *is* a case for a fundamental re-examination of the social security system 40 years after the Beveridge Report. Such an exercise, however, must be comprehensive enough to include the structure of tax reliefs and allowances which privileges the better-off, and the endemic problem of low pay which penalises women in particular. It must be an 'open review' in nature as well as in name; if fundamental principles are being re-examined, then they must be re-examined in public and with due notice, not sprung on participants or discussed only by a small group of civil servants in secret. Above all, those giving evidence, and the public in general, must be allowed adequate time to consider and debate the crucial issues involved.

The government's social security reviews of 1984 fulfil none of these criteria. Norman Fowler may be keen to go down in history as a second William Beveridge. However, in practice, the short-term dictates of crisis management within the DHSS have been combined uneasily with a longer-term project of changing the parameters of debate about social security, to fit a more limited set of objectives. The hybrid end product will, at best, be merely the starting-point for the more thorough, comprehensive and open debate which CPAG, amongst many others, considers essential.

References

1 Minister responsible for commissioning the Beveridge Report, *House of Commons Hansard*, 16 February 1943, col 16/8, quoted in A W Dilnot, J A Kay and C N Morris, *The Reform of Social Security*, IFS 1984, p 9.
2 Dr Rhodes Boyson (then Minister for Social Security), introducing the first session of oral evidence for the review of benefits for children and young people on 9 July 1984.
3 See, for example, *House of Commons Hansard*, 2 April 1984, cols 652-60.
4 See Chapter 1, esp pp 7-13.
5 Letter from Dr Rhodes Boyson to CPAG, 1 May 1984.
6 As note 5.
7 *The Times*, 5 April 1984.
8 *The Times*, 4 April 1984.
9 See *Poverty*, CPAG journal, April 1983, p 3.
10 See, for example, bulletins from the National Campaign Against Social Security Cuts.
11 Joint letter from Age Concern, CHAR, CPAG, Disability Alliance, FSU, FWA, LPU, NCOPF, RADAR and Youthaid to the Secretary of State for Social Services, 3 May 1984 (press-released on 8 May 1984). Joint letter to *The Times* from NCVO, CPAG, Age Concern, Spastics Society, NACAB, Family Forum and LPU, written on 26 June 1984.
12 The reviews of supplementary benefit and benefits for children and young people were announced on 2 April 1984 in the House of Commons by Norman Fowler, Secretary of State for Social Services (*House of Commons Hansard*, 2 April 1984, cols 652-60).
13 Some of the major themes in the written evidence to the reviews were summarised in *Poverty*, CPAG journal, Winter 1984/85, pp 25-35.
14 CPAG's evidence to the reviews, *1984: Changed Priorities Ahead?*, is available from CPAG at £3.25 (for the full volume) or £1.25 each for the separate submissions to the reviews of benefits for children and young people, supplementary benefit and housing benefit.
15 See note 12 above.
16 Evidence from CPAG to the review of benefits for children and young people, August 1984 (see note 14 above).
17 See note 12 above.
18 In 'The Taxation of Husband and Wife: a view of the debate in the Green Paper' (June 1982), John Kay and Catherine Sandler analysed 37

submissions to the government's Green Paper on the taxation of husband and wife, and found that 20 of these favoured introducing a system of independent taxation for husbands and wives, and using the money to increase cash benefits, including child benefit.

19 *Daily Telegraph*, 4 April 1984.

20 See Louie Burghes and Ray Stagles, *No Choice at 16: a study of educational maintenance allowances*, CPAG 1983.

21 Evidence from CPAG to the housing benefit review, August 1984 (see note 14 above). An edited version of our submission has been published in a collection of 16 submissions to the housing benefit review: *Housing Benefit: the evidence*, the Housing Centre Trust, 33 Alfred Place, London WC1 (£7.50).

22 Consultation document for the housing benefit review, issued on 16 May 1984 by the DHSS.

23 Consultation document for the supplementary benefit review, issued on 16 May 1984 by the DHSS.

24 Evidence from CPAG to the supplementary benefit review, August 1984 (see note 14 above).

25 See Ruth Lister, *Social Assistance: the real challenge*, CPAG 1978, and *The No-Cost, No-Benefit Review*, CPAG 1979.

26 See note 23 above.

27 See J Allbeson and R Smith, *We don't give clothing grants any more*, CPAG 1984; R Berthoud, *The Reform of Supplementary Benefit: working papers*, Policy Studies Institute 1984; G Beltram, *Testing the Safety Net: an enquiry into the reformed supplementary benefit scheme*, Bedford Square Press 1984. See also *Poverty*, Winter 1984/85, pp 16-24, in which David Bull reviews these and other pieces of research into the post-1980 SB scheme.

28 See CPAG's pre-Budget memorandum for 1984, and bulletins from the Unemployment Alliance (a group of voluntary organisations of which CPAG is a member).

29 See note 12 above.

30 See Allbeson and Smith, note 27 above; and Tamar Raphael and Jo Roll, *Carrying the Can: charities and the welfare state*, CPAG/Family Welfare Association 1984.

31 From the summary of CPAG's evidence to the SB review (see note 24 above).

32 See note 31 above.

33 Lynda Chalker (then DHSS parliamentary under-secretary), *House of Commons Hansard*, 6 November 1979, col 168W (quoting from SBC Annual Report, 1978).

34 During their oral evidence, the Association of Metropolitan Authorities, the Adam Smith Institute, the Trades Union Congress and CPAG itself all called for an enquiry of this sort.

35 *Poverty*, August 1984, pp 38-40.

36 See, for example, 'From the Cradle to the Grave', evidence submitted jointly to the reviews by the DHSS trade unions SCPS and CPSA; 'Curbing Leviathan', by the Association of British Chambers of Commerce, June 1984.

37 *Sunday Times*, 8 April 1984.

38 Judith Walpole, 'Current social security issues', *Politics Today*, No 17, 8 October 1984.

39 *The Times*, 4 April 1984, article by Sarah Hogg, economics editor.

40 *Financial Times*, 26 November 1984, article by Peter Riddell, political editor.

41 Joint letter to *The Times*, 26 June 1984 (see note 11 above).

42 Oral evidence sessions of the review of benefits for children and young people in July, August and September 1984, chaired by Dr Rhodes Boyson and later by Norman Fowler (unpublished).
43 *Daily Telegraph*, 10 October 1984.
44 *The Reform of Social Security* (see note 1 above); *Of Benefit to All*, National Consumer Council 1984; Peter Ashby, *Social Security After Beveridge: what next?*, Bedford Square Press/NCVO 1984.
45 See 'Towards a new social income', written for National Consumer Council's review of the social security system (see note 44 above); and *Poverty*, Winter 1984/85, pp 36-43.
46 *Social Security After Beveridge* (see note 44 above), pp 18-19; *The Reform of Social Security* (see note 1 above), pp 114-15.
47 See *Into the Twenty-First Century: the development of social security*, ILO 1984, which makes a similar point about governments' criticisms of growing expenditure on social security.
48 Rory O'Kelly, 'Why social dividends are not the answer', *Policy Studies*, Vol 5, Part 2, October 1984, p 29.
49 Michael Prowse, *Financial Times*, 30 August 1984.
50 See note 49 above.
51 *Guardian*, 17 January 1985.
52 *New Society*, 27 October 1984, interview with Norman Fowler.
53 Treasury and Civil Service Committee, *The Structure of Personal Income Taxation and Income Support*, HC Paper 386, 1982-93.

Appendix: the social security reviews 1984

Comment from CHILD POVERTY ACTION GROUP*

Whilst CPAG welcomes the opportunity to submit written and oral evidence to the social security reviews, we wish to express our concern about the format and context of the reviews in general. We are therefore submitting this appendix to each of the review teams.

1 *Timetable and agenda for public consultation*
We are concerned that the reviews should provide genuine opportunities for public debate and consultation. A 'great debate' on the welfare state cannot be conducted in a hurry. We were therefore concerned to note that the consultation documents were not issued until six weeks after the announcement of the two most recent reviews; and that the deadline for written evidence was set a mere ten weeks after that. The review teams are to report by the end of 1984, and the government's proposals for reform are to be published shortly afterwards.

An open and thorough debate on the crucial questions facing the welfare state some 40 years after the Beveridge Report cannot be conducted in an over-hasty manner. *We urge the government to reconsider its timetable for public consultation, and to extend it.*

We are also anxious about the piecemeal and confused nature of the agenda for debate. The secretary of state has claimed that the reviews amount to 'the most substantial examination of the social security system since the Beveridge Report'. Yet, on the surface at least, the review teams will not even be examining the whole social security system, not to mention personal taxation. In particular, there seems to be undue emphasis on means-tested benefits considered in isolation from the non-means-tested elements of social security provision such as national insurance benefits.

Press reports have, however, suggested that the issues under consideration are much wider, and the proposals for reform much more sweeping, than the consultation documents indicate. Whilst we would welcome a wide-ranging debate, it should not take place behind closed doors. We therefore urge the government to *give a clear and definitive list of the issues under consideration.*

* This is a shortened version of an Appendix which CPAG sent to each of the review teams with its written evidence, August 1984.

2 *An open and unbiased debate: public documents*
The Minister for Social Security has announced that the government will produce a paper 'of some colour' after considering the reports from the review teams. We urge the government to *give a clear assurance that such a document will be a Green rather than a White Paper.* Opportunities for consultation on any proposed reforms are essential in order that an open and unbaised debate can take place. Moving immediately from separate reviews to a White Paper or a Bill would be seen as unacceptable by a wide range of organisations.

We also again urge the government to *publish both the written and the oral evidence given to the reviews.* In previous exercises of a similar nature, the evidence presented has provided valuable information, and its publication has at least indicated to the public that an open consultation is desired by the government.

3 *The aims of the reviews*
The consultation documents describe the reviews as 'a substantial re-examination of the social security system to see if better use can be made of resources and staff within the present overall level of social security expenditure'. We are disturbed to note this *imposition of an arbitrary financial ceiling*, for several reasons. First, it takes no account of the substantial reductions in the social security budget since 1979 now amounting to an estimated cumulative total of over £6½ billion (*The Times*, 25 June 1984). A large proportion of these 'savings' has been achieved by the government's decision to break the link between increases in average earnings and the upratings of long-term benefits, thus ending any hope nurtured by social security beneficiaries of sharing in the rising living standards of the rest of the community. Yet £4.17 billion is being 'given away' this tax year alone due to income tax changes (over and above indexation) during the government's first and second terms of office. The top 1 per cent of taxpayers is getting 44 per cent of this total, whilst the bottom 25 per cent have only 3 per cent to share between them (*House of Commons Hansard*, 4 April 1984, cols 542-4). These figures exclude the £860m given to the better-off through changes in capital taxes over and above indexation over the same period (*House of Commons Hansard*, 17 May 1984, cols 238-9). *To suggest that the review teams, and those giving evidence to them, should not query the application of priorities which has led to these changes, or suggest a change in such priorities, seems to indicate an artificial narrowing of a crucial area of debate.*

Second, although the review teams should look wider than the social security budget alone for resources to finance reform, *some resources are available within the social security budget itself.* The latest statistics, covering 1981 or 1981/82, suggest that at least £900m of social security benefits went unclaimed; the total must by now be considerably higher. These unclaimed resources should be considered as part of the total available within the social security budget.

Moreover, the review teams should also examine the *present methods of financing social security* in any consideration of a more equitable framework. Removal of the regressive 'ceiling' on liability for national insurance contributions, for example, would raise an estimated additional £1,270m in this tax year alone (*House of Commons Hansard*, 15 March 1984, col 272) to finance improvements to social security provision.

Third, there is no mention of the *'hidden welfare state' of tax reliefs* and privileges, which, in practice, have the same impact on total public expenditure as increases in the social security budget, but are not included in the public spending totals. Since one important aim of the reviews is to 'channel [the available resources] to where they are most needed', the 'resources available' in, for example, mortgage interest tax relief and the married man's tax allowance (which are of more value to those on higher incomes) should be included in the debate.

Fourth, whilst it is a laudable aim 'to ascertain whether we can simplify the system' of social security benefits, *the lessons of previous attempts at simplification within a nil-cost remit should be learned*. The reform of supplementary benefit in 1980 and the introduction of housing benefit in 1982-3 left millions of claimants worse off, without notable advances in simplicity for claimants or staff. The available evidence suggests overwhelmingly that *benefit levels are inadequate*, particularly for families with children, and that *beneficiaries cannot afford any further reductions*. The complications of the present structure are largely due to over-reliance on means-tested benefits, owing to the failure of successive governments to commit sufficient resources to achieve Beveridge's aim of 'security against want without a means test'. This failure should not be visited on claimants again, as it has so often been in the past.

4 *Conclusion*

The 'crisis' of welfare expenditure predicted by the Think Tank Report in 1982 appears to have been exaggerated. The government's recent Green Paper was also more optimistic about economic growth, though it suggested that extra resources would be used primarily for tax cuts, rather than for an effective anti-poverty strategy. As we said in our 1984 pre-Budget memorandum:

> Any debate about the future of the welfare state must make

> clear that decisions about the balance between public spending and taxation involve political choices. . . We believe there is a case for such a debate provided the right issues are addressed. One of these issues . . . is the extent of poverty in this country. The welfare state has failed in one of its prime purposes — to abolish want. How to tackle the growing problem of poverty is one of the most important questions, if not the most important, facing the welfare state today. (pp 26-7)

We believe that to tackle this 'growing problem' there should be a system of adequate non-means-tested benefits; the means-tested route to the abolition of poverty has failed. Higher child benefits are an essential starting-point for any more rational and equitable system of income distribution. A programme to tackle low pay, and a more progressive tax system, are also essential elements of a coherent anti-poverty strategy.

Whilst the reviews could constitute the first step in the debate about developing an effective strategy to eliminate poverty, such a debate cannot be either open or unbiased unless these points about the form and content of the reviews are taken into account.

Racism and Social Security / No 67
Paul Gordon
Looks at how racism operates in the social security system. It examines the connections between immigration law and the welfare state, and how the DHSS operates a form of internal immigration control and fails to serve the interests of minority groups.
c 95pp £2.95 0 903963 86 8
Joint publication: CPAG and Runnymede Trust April 1985

Families Rent Apart / No 65
Shirley Cusack and Jo Roll
Introduction by Paul Lewis
In April 1984, the contributions many young people had to make to their parents' housing costs rose dramatically, as a result of cuts in the housing benefit scheme. This pamphlet investigates the harsh consequences for families.
36pp £1.95 0 903963 85 X
Joint publication: CPAG and Youthaid April 1985

Round about 50 hours a week / No 64
David Piachaud
Parenthood takes a lot of time which, if valued, works out as £200 a week for a family with a child under 5. Piachaud discusses child care and the need for increased child benefit to recognise the time costs of child care.
30pp £1.75 0 903963 82 5 December 1984

Carrying the Can / No 63
Tamar Raphael and Jo Roll
Charities are increasingly asked to help pay for basic necessities when families can't live on their social security benefits. In particular the pamphlet looks at the demands made on the Family Welfare Association for help with clothing grants.
24pp £1.50 0 903963 81 7 August 1984
Joint publication: CPAG and Family Welfare Association

'We don't give clothing grants any more' / No 62
Janet Allbeson and Roger Smith
An examination of the 1980 supplementary benefit reform and the ensuing impact on the quality of service given to claimants. *'Highly readable... despatched from the frontline'* Legal Action Bulletin
114pp £2.50 0 903963 73 6 April 1984

Rights Guide for Homeowners
5th edition
Jo Tunnard and Clare Whately
Revised by Beth Lakani and Lorraine Thompson
Aimed at homeowners on a tight budget, the guide gives practical advice on how to keep a home by cutting costs and increasing income. It looks at ways of negotiating with local authorities and building societies, if there are mortgage arrears, and how to meet repair bills.
120pp £2.50 0 903963 84 1 March 1985
Joint publication: CPAG and SHAC

Round about 40 pence a week